Lessons to Nourish the Soul: Luke

By

Rev. Marjorie E. Palmer

Table of Contents

Luke 1: 47-55

47and my spirit has begun to rejoice in
God my Savior,
48 because he has looked upon the
humble state of his servant.
For from now on all generations will
call me blessed,
49 because he who is mighty has done
great things for me, and holy is his
name;
50 from generation to
generation he is merciful to
those who fear him.
51 He has demonstrated power with his
arm; he has scattered those whose
pride wells up from the sheer
arrogance of their hearts.
52 He has brought down the mighty
from their thrones, and has lifted
up those of lowly position;
53 he has filled the hungry with good
things, and has sent the rich away
empty.
54 He has helped his servant Israel,
remembering his mercy,
55 as he promised to our ancestors, to
Abraham and to his descendants
forever."

'<u>I LIFT UP MY SOUL</u>'

I heard a funny story the other day. You know computers are wonderful things … most of the time. They do have their glitches, but they are mostly wonderful. I'm sure it would be much, much harder to do a lot of the work I do, if I didn't have a computer to use.

Apparently there was a church secretary of a Catholic church who was getting used to some of the features on her computer. She had just learned how to use the find/replace mode on her word processor. She discovered that she could search for a word and change that for a different word. In fact, she could find all the same word and make a 'universal' change to all the same names in the document.

One of the things the secretary did was make bulletins for Mass and for funerals. Apparently a woman named Mary had died and she had made up the bulletin for her funeral. A week later Edna died. Another bulletin was required for that funeral. So, thought the secretary, I can use my 'universal replace' button and make all that work very easy. So she did.

When the people at the funeral service had the bulletin in hand, however, they were surprised to see the Holy Virgin Edna in one of the prayers!

Today we are looking at the Magnificat, Mary's Song. It is one of the most well-known and loved Scriptures in the Bible. Yet it may be that Mary's song presents a problem to us

Protestants, and therefore, we may miss the message in her Song.

The problem arises because the subject of Mary is a sensitive one, which has divided Catholics and Protestants for many years.

This comes from various myths that have developed about Mary.

The greatest of these myths is a myth that the virgin birth is a myth. I can see how atheists, who do not believe in God, would think that a virgin birth is scientifically impossible and therefore impossible to have happened. But, as the Anger Gabriel told Mary, "with God nothing is impossible." If God can create an entire universe from nothing, then begetting a child in the womb of a virgin can't be that much harder. The virgin birth is not a myth.

Sometimes we hear people say that St. Mary healed them from some disease. There are thousands of people who make a pilgrimage each year to Mary's shrine in Lourdes, France, seeking healing. Any many people are healed there. But Mary is not the source of healing; God is. God is always the healer, no matter what the vehicle of healing is— doctors, medicine, surgery, prayer— God is the healer.

Some have tried to suggest that Mary belongs in a category by herself, that she should be put on a pedestal, elevated above all humans. But Jesus, himself, said otherwise. In Luke we read that someone had called to Jesus: "Blessed is the womb that bore you and the breasts that you sucked.!" But Jesus returned: 'Bless rather are those who hear the Word of God and keep it." At another time (recorded in Luke 8:19-21) "His mother and his brothers come to Him, but they could not reach Him for the crowd. And he was told, 'Your mother and your brothers are standing outside, desiring to see you,' but Jesus said to them, 'My mother and my brothers are those who hear the Word of God and do it."

Jesus was fairly blunt in both of these instances, and there is no indication that Mary should be placed in a class by herself.

There are other myths about Mary that have grown up over the centuries. They take away from the person and work of Jesus and attribute to Mary what we should only attribute to her son. Some even go so far as to describe Mary as co-redeemer of the world with Jesus. That is, she was responsible as much as Jesus for the salvation of the world. That is sheer blasphemy! (Munro) (I read an article about that a couple of years about in Newsweek. Just because some magazine prints such an article doesn't make it so!

One of the hottest arguments that the church fought was about calling Mary the *theotokos,* the Mother of God. When I was young, calling Mary the Mother of God made me feel very strange. It seemed to elevate Mary far beyond being human. But back in the 4th Century, one of the Ancient Church Councils voted that, indeed, Mary is the *theotokos,* the bearer of God, because that designation speaks about who Jesus is. Jesus is the Christ, and Mary bore him.

Calling Mary the Mother of God doesn't elevate her beyond humanity, it speaks of whom Christ is—God taking on flesh and living among us to redeem us.

The song of Mary is known as The Magnificat.

Mary did not actually sing the words, but they radiated her love, her joy and her pleasure in being asked to participate in the heavenly scheme that would bring salvation to this world.

It's hard to imagine, to really put ourselves in Mary's shoes, so to speak. Even though I am a woman and share women's issues with Mary, our social situations today and back then are quite different.

Girls were not educated the same way boys were. They didn't read or write. They were taught the critical business of homemaking, working a garden, preparing the meals, baking the bread; retrieving the water from the community well, tending the children, weaving and sewing all the clothes anyone in the family would need, washing, and cleaning. Life for a young woman would have revolved around the home and tending and caring for it and its members.

That's not to say that females were not informed about their faith. The faith was taught to them, too. They heard the stories of the God of Abraham, the God of Isaac, and the God of Jacob. They knew the prophecy that was made to King David, that one of his seed would sit on a throne that would have no end. That son would be the King forever and ever. Mary would have known that prophecy. All young Jewish women knew that prophecy, and they knew that some young woman would be the mother of such a King. (It might have been the secret dream of every young woman that she might be that special person to be the mother of such a

King.)

It was traditional for a young woman to be betrothed in marriage when she came of age, which was usually around 13 or 14 years old. So Mary was betrothed to Joseph, a carpenter of the village. He was several years older than Mary, maybe in his late twenties. Their betrothal was a binding contract, just like a marriage contract, but their union would not be consummated until the wedding. That was all done according to tradition.

St. Luke tells us that one night Mary was visited by an Angel, the Angel Gabriel. He told her of God's plan to place the heavenly child within her womb and make her the mother of God's child. That must have been an incredible moment. Mary wondered, *"How can this be since I am a virgin?"* And Gabriel assured her saying, *"The Holy Spirit will come upon you, and the power of the Most High will overshadow you; therefore, the child to be born will be holy; he will be called the Son of God."* Gabriel told Mary that her cousin Elizabeth had also conceived in her old age and would bear a son, even though she had been barren. Gabriel added, *"for with God nothing is impossible."* Then Mary spoke: *"Here am I, the servant of the Lord; let it be with me according to your word."*

Scripture is silent on the next happenings. We don't know what happened just following the angel's visit to Mary's. Did she confide in her mom and dad? Did she talk to Joseph, her betrothed? Luke tells us that she made haste to travel to the hill country in Judea where her cousin Elizabeth and Zechariah lived.

Now Judea isn't near Nazareth, it's some 60 miles away. Mary must have made some arrangements to travel so far. Perhaps she knew some folks who were on their way to Jerusalem and she could accompany them. (I can't see how she could have made her way alone that far. It would have been socially inappropriate.)

Mary had some time to think about her mysterious visitor and the even more mysterious message that the angel brought. She was familiar with the prophecy about the Messiah. Gabriel had told her that the child she would bear "… *will be great, and will be called the Son of the Most High, and the Lord God will give to him the throne of his ancestor David. He will reign over the house of Jacob forever, and of his kingdom there will be no end."*

Those were such wonderful words. Yes! The Israelites had been waiting for such a one to come. They were looking for him to come. They treasured the promise of his arrival in their hearts. If truth be known, every young Israelite girl thought, "what if I am the one who would bear such a child? What if I am the one chosen to be the mother of the Messiah? What an honor that would be!"

"Could this really be so? Thought Mary. "Am I really the one? Did I really hear right? Was Gabriel's visit real, or was it just a dream that came in the night?" But the angel had told Mary something else, something that would confirm his words. He told her that her cousin Elizabeth was with child even in her advanced years. So Mary decided to visit her.

Mary's mind must have been set awhirl. So

many thoughts were all bound together. Being with child! Being the chosen one! The Angel's visit. The honor of it all. And then more down to earth matters. What would her parents say? What about Joseph? How could she explain this to him? What would the neighbors think?

Mary couldn't stop thinking all the way up to Elizabeth's house. Every step she took was filled with a mix of excitement, thrill, and a little panic.

Mary must have been a person of strong faith. She had learned her prayers at her mother's knees and she never missed them. She knew by heart every story of her people from Father Abraham, to Moses and the escape from slavery, the wonder of the Law, King David, the dreadful exile in Babylon, the rebuilding of Jerusalem and the temple. Mary especially loved the Psalms, most of which she could recite by memory. She could sing many of them. I'll bet she had a pretty voice, one that would sing many melodies to her infant son.

I can imagine Mary singing the psalm we call the twenty-fifth Psalm.

> Unto thee O Lord, I lift up
> my soul Unto thee O Lord,
> I lift up my soul O my God,
> I trust in thee,
>
> Let me not be afraid,
>
> Let not my enemies triumph over me.

And she loved to hear the stories of the Israelite women like Sarah, Hannah and Ruth.

Mary had no idea what was about to happen. She had no idea what it would be like to give birth to her first child in a place far from her home, far from her family, in a strange place, without any help.

She had no idea the fear she would feel when she and her new husband and son would have to flee for their very lives to Egypt in the dead of night.

She had no idea the wonder of being the mother of a remarkable child, growing in stature and in favor with God and men. She had no idea the pride she would feel as she would watch her young son begin to learn the trade of his earthly father, and begin to create beautiful things from the wood shop.

Mary had no idea what it would be like to be the mother of the most wonderful preacher and teacher in their land. She had no idea how marvelous it would be to see him heal many, many people of their pains and diseases.

Mary could have no idea the pain, the grief, the absolute horror she would feel when she would stand at her son's feet as he hung, bleeding to death on the cross.

No, Mary would have no idea about any of those things. Mary would have been firmly grounded in her faith in what her God had done and what her God was able to do. Mary was all about being willing to participate in whatever way she could. Whatever God was asking her was okay with Mary. Mary trusted

God. –*O my God, I trust in thee, Let me not be afraid, let not my enemies triumph over me.*

All these thoughts spun round in her head as she walked along her journey. Then finally, she had arrived. As she approached her cousin's house, Elizabeth saw her and exclaimed:

> "*Blessed are you among women, and blessed is the fruit of your womb. And why has this happened to me, that the mother of my Lord comes to me? For as soon as I heard the sound of your greeting, the child in my womb leaped for joy. And blessed is she who believed that there would be a fulfillment of what was spoken to her by the Lord.*"

Then Mary spoke:

> "*My soul magnifies the Lord, and my spirit rejoices in God my Savior, for he has looked with favor on the lowliness of his servant.*
>
> *Surely, from now on all generations will call me blessed; for the Mighty One has done great things for me, and holy is his name.*
>
> *His mercy is for those who fear him from generation to generation.*
>
> *He has shown strength with his arm; he has scattered the proud in the thoughts of their hearts.*
>
> *He has brought down the powerful from*

their thrones, and lifted up the lowly;

*he has filled the hungry with good things,
and sent the rich away empty.*

*He has helped his servant Israel, in
remembrance of his mercy, according to
the promise he made to our ancestors, to
Abraham and to his descendants
forever."*

Mary's words have echoed down to us through the
ages. We could dissect this beautiful hymn into
careful bites and dig into each section, but this
morning I would like us to think of it in its entirety as
a beautiful statement of Mary's faith, which is
completely wrapped up in love for her LORD.

The first words of Mary's Song set the spirit of the
whole. Mary is filled with joy as she exclaims: *My
soul magnifies the LORD, and my spirit rejoices in
God my Savior."*

Mary had come to trust and have complete
confidence in whatever has been set before her
on this amazing adventure.

She didn't know all that would be involved.
Would become an act of worship. It was an
outward expression of her inward spirit. Her
whole being sang praise to God for what was
happening in her life.

That's what we can learn from Mary's Song.
When we realize what God is doing in our lives
and praise him for it, we have begun true
worship.

Magnify is a term that isn't obvious to
understand. It sounds good, but what does it

actually mean?

Mary is referring to herself in her most basic form, her soul. That part of her that comes from God and belongs to God. Her soul is who she is -- her deepest, most intimate part of her (could she have said the bottom of her heart? It's about the same thing.)

> My soul magnifies the Lord.

> My soul makes great or shines for the Lord.

Some translations help us by saying glorifies instead of magnifies. I remember Jesus using that word in the Sermon on the Mount. Jesus was telling his disciples to let their light shine, to become conspicuous with their faith. To do good works for others that would reflect on God. Because then, Jesus said, people would see your good works and give glory to God.

So that helps, I think. We glorify God when we do what God wants us to do, when we follow God's will.

And of course, that's what Mary had just done. She had been willing to work as a junior partner with God in God's plan of salvation. She had told the Angel that she was the servant of the Lord, and that she was willing to participate in whatever God had in mind for her to do.

> My soul magnifies the Lord.

> And my spirit rejoices in God my savior.

Mary not only was willing to participate in God's

plan, but sh embraced it wholeheartedly. She rejoiced in it.

There's another verse in Psalms, one that I love to sing, that goes;

> 'Delight yourself in the Lord, and he will give you the desires of your heart.'

It goes to a little tune—"Delight yourself in the Lord, Delight yourself in the Lord, and He will give you the desires of your heart, and he will give you the desires of your heart. "

Tunes help me remember words.

It's really a circular logic thing. You know you start here at the top of the circle. "Delight yourself in the Lord." That's all about learning about God, about learning God's plan, and God's plan for your life, and then delighting in it. Delight yourself (we don't say that too often, please yourself with what God is about. Make God's will your will, too.

Then God will be happy to give you what you desire, because it matches up with his will. Of course you will get the desires of your heart, because that's exactly what God wants for you to have. (The circle is complete.)

Mary said her spirit rejoiced in God, her savior.

She had made God's will her will, too, and she was rejoicing in it. She felt that she was ready for whatever was coming her way. She felt safe, knowing that she was in the center of God's will. (*yea, though I walk through the valley of the shadow of death I will fear no evil, thy rod and thy staff, they comfort me.*—I rejoice in God's will)

Mary is a perfect example of Christian discipleship. I think she really is the first disciple, and that's why she has been so loved over all these years.

Her life and her commitment ask us a great question. Are we following Jesus, our Lord and Savior? Are we magnifying him by doing good works, by being conspicuous Christians in our world? Do people see our good works and know that they come from our love of the LORD?

Do we delight in God our savior? Do we delight in his ways and make them our own? Or do we think first of what we want, regardless of what God is telling us to do?

Luke 3: 1-6

3 In the fifteenth year of the reign of Tiberius Caesar, when Pontius Pilate was governor of Judea, and Herod was tetrarch of Galilee, and his brother Philip was tetrarch of the region of Iturea and Trachonitis, and Lysanias was tetrarch of Abilene, 2 during the high priesthood of Annas and Caiaphas, the word of God came to John the son of Zechariah in the wilderness. 3 He went into all the region around the Jordan River, preaching a baptism of repentance for the forgiveness of sins.

4 As it is written in the book of the words of Isaiah the prophet,

"The voice of one shouting in the wilderness: 'Prepare the way for the Lord, make his paths straight.

5 Every valley will be filled,

and every mountain and hill will be brought low, and the crooked will be made straight, and the rough ways will be made smooth,

6 and all humanity will see the salvation of God.'"

<u>PREPARING THE HEART</u>

"Prepare ye the way of the Lord….."   from Godspell

Prepare! That was John the Baptist's message. Prepare ye the way of the Lord!

We find ourselves preparing for all sorts of things in this world. In fact, if we thought about it, we'd discover that nearly everything we do involves some sort of preparation. Some preparations cost … even quite a lot. People who get into professions have years and years of preparation and many dollars spent getting to the final spot of being doctor or lawyer or pastor. We prepare in so many ways.

This month is all about preparing for Christmas. That's what Advent is about—preparing. You've been looking at the church and noticing the changes.

We've got a wonderful crèche' outside—the stable with Mary and Joseph and the Baby and the Kings and the critters all lit up. Everyone who drives by can see those preparations.

We've got the tree with all the pretty Chrismons on it. I don't know if you've ever spent any time looking at the Chrismons, but each of them took time and effort to hand make for our tree. I wonder how many years we've had the Chrismons?

The Advent wreathe and the candles in the windows and all the poinsettias…they all took preparations to get them here and to display.

And that's just here at church. I'd be willing to bet that many of you have already put up a tree at home. And maybe you've been out buying gifts for Christmas. How about doing the Christmas cards? Is anyone here finished sending out your cards? Then there's Christmas! Preparations have to be done for it, too.

There's the dinner, which may involve having special guests. You have to write up a menu and start cooking the pies and breads and cranberries and all that ahead of time. All those things are part of the preparation for Christmas.

Why do you suppose we prepare for Christmas? Is that what John the Baptist was talking about when he preached that we have to prepare ye the way of the Lord? Do you think? Do you think he'd be surprised if he walked through Madison Square Mall today in preparation for the coming of the King?

Our Scripture today comes from Luke, chapter 3 verses 1-6:

[1]*In the fifteenth year of the reign of Emperor Tiberius, when Pontius Pilate was governor of Judea, and Herod was ruler   of Galilee, and his brother Philip ruler of the region of Ituraea and Trachonitis, and Lysanias ruler of Abilene,* [2]*during the high priesthood of Annas and Caiaphas, the word of God came to John son of Zechariah in the wilderness.* [3]*He went into all the region around the Jordan, proclaiming a baptism of repentance for the*

forgiveness of sins, *⁴as it is written in the book of the words of the prophet Isaiah,*

"The voice of one crying out in the wilderness:

'Prepare the way of the Lord, make his paths straight.

⁵ *Every valley shall be filled,*

and every mountain and hill shall be made low, and the crooked shall be made straight, and the rough ways made smooth; ⁶ and all flesh shall see the salvation of God.'"

John was not an average man. He was different from the average man. He didn't live in the community; he lived out in the desert, east of the towns. He lived alone and he ate wild honey and locusts and wore a camel's hair shirt. That would scratch forever! He definitely was not an ordinary man. God had called John for a very special task. He was to prepare the people for the coming of the Messiah, the King of the Jews.

John preached to the people and called them to be baptized in the river Jordan as a sign of their repentance and the forgiveness of their sins.

John cried—*prepare ye the way of the LORD!* John was not talking about preparing for the

Christmas season. He was talking about another kind of preparation, one that happens in our hearts not something that we can buy on line or pick up at Wal-Mart.

St. Luke tells us that John was the one whom the Prophet Isaiah wrote--

One who was a voice crying in the wilderness— "Prepare ye the way of the Lord. Make straight the pathways, pull down the mountains and raise the valleys. Make the way easy for the LORD to travel on.

This picture is like saying roll out the red carpet! Make the way beautiful and welcoming to the King when he comes.

Have you ever seen how the President is welcomed? They roll out the red carpet for him when he steps out of the plane. And that's true for brides, too. Before the bride comes down the aisle, a red carpet is rolled out before her, preparing the way for her, making it clean and dry and gracious for the bride to walk upon.

"Prepare ye the way of the Lord."

The preparation that John was talking about was repenting. He called the people to repent of their sins and be baptized as a sign of the change.

Apparently, our hearts in their natural condition are very unwelcoming to God. Our hearts have all sorts of hills and valleys inside that keep God out.

That difficult terrain is another way of saying that we are sinful people, doing our own thing, not listening to our maker not listening to God.

John called us to repentance to make a change in our lives.

When we hear something like that there are some steps that can we can walk through to evaluate it.

First, we need to consider if there is a need.

Second, we need to count the cost.

Once these two questions have been answered to our satisfaction, we can move ahead and make the decision.

What sort of need would John be addressing that he seems to think we need to remedy?

John is talking about forgiveness of our sins. We have to look at our lives and discover if there is anything to this. Am I a sinful person? If so, is that a big deal? Do I need a savior?

There isn't a person here that can truthfully admit to being sinless. Every one of us is sinful. We can't probably get through an entire day without sinning in some way. St. Paul tells us so in Romans 3:23—For all have sinned and fallen short of the glory of God.

If you're not sure, think of your relationships— your spouse, your kids, your folks, your family, your boss, your subordinates. Are you in complete harmony with each of them? Do you owe anyone an apology for your hot temper or your foolish words?

Have we ever said more than we should about someone else? Have we ever caused pain to someone because of our angry tongue? Have we struck at someone and hurt them? Have we ever lied and lied again to cover the first lie?

How about the other side of pain? Have we

been the recipient of someone's abuse? Have we not forgiven that person? Do we hold a grudge against someone who has hurt us or spoken unkindly to us or purposefully damaged us?

How about our most important relationship? The relationship with our God? Do we live thankfully every day? Have we remembered to take all our fears and pains to God and to leave them there? Do we trust God for our very lives and every aspect of our lives? Do we believe that all things work together for good because we have been called according to God's purpose? (Rom 8:28)

If you are answering, "yes" to these questions, even one of them, you have begun to realize that we are sinners and we have a need for repentance.

By the way, repentance is not about being sorry for something. Contrition is important, being sorry for our misdoings, but true repentance is more than just being sorry, it's about changing from the wrong and moving toward what's right. Repentance is changing the mind from this to that. Repentance is about changing the DEFAULT position in our heart from being a ME-CENTERED person to being a GOD-CENTERED person. That means that when we interact with others we think that as we act to the other we are acting toward our God. (In as much as you do it for the least of my family members you do it to me. (Matt. 25: 40)

So perhaps we have become convinced that this business of repentance has some merit. We need to repent, but.... Don't do it yet!

When we make an important change in our lives we need to count the cost before we jump into the program, before we put down the earnest money or sign the contract.

And there are some very important costs associated with repenting. I don't think pastors regularly preach about the cost of repenting, because lots of pastors want to get the people on their knees first and ask questions later. That's not fair. We need to be very aware up front of the costs. Like the truth in lending laws in contracts today. We need to read the fine print, so to speak.

What fine print? I thought that Jesus' love and salvation is free? Isn't it free? Why do we hear it's free if there's some cost associated with it?

Good question! Yes! Indeed! Jesus' salvation is free! There's nothing we can do to merit God's love or our salvation. But even so, it's ours for the taking.

That is the Good News! (Remember Rom. 5:8—*God shows his love for us, for while we were yet sinners Christ died for us.*)

We need to count the cost of our discipleship— the cost of our following Jesus before we make that decision. We need to be aware that following Jesus expects that there will be changes, significant changes, in your life. When you come to a relationship with Jesus it is not like joining a club.

Jesus spoke about the cost of discipleship. He asked, *"for which of you, intending to build a tower, does not first sit down and estimate the cost, to see whether he has enough to complete it? Otherwise, when he has laid a foundation and is not able to finish, all who see it will begin to ridicule him, saying, 'This fellow began to build and was not able to finish.' Or what king, going out to wage war against another king, will not sit down first and consider whether he is able with ten thousand to oppose the one who comes against him with twenty thousand? If he cannot, then, while the other is still far away, he sends a delegation and asks for the terms of peace.* (Luke 14:28-32)

Repentance will cost us something. In fact, it will cost us a great deal.

God's invitation to come to him is completely free, but the cost to us once we've accepted the invitation is quite a different matter.

You see God is calling us to reorder our lives in a new way that will allow us to grow in God's love.

That reordering is a tall order, because it will reach into every portion of our lives and it will cause us to change our habits, gradually calling us to purify our intentions in everything we do. This is not a small price; it is an enormous price; it is the price of your whole life and all that you do. It involves giving everything of yours back to God, making your whole life available for God's use.

The biggest cost to us is our pride. We have no need for selfish pride, the pride that says I'm right and you're wrong. The pride that says "I'm worth it" or "I deserve it" just like the T.V. ads are saying these days. Pride that says I won't forgive someone; I won't humble myself to do forgive him/her.

You could say that we have a natural default position to always consider ourselves first, always put our own gain before anyone else. That way of thinking has to change when we become Christian. We have to change the default position—that is the first position. We have to begin to look at the world through God's eyes, which means considering you, yes, but also considering all of God's other children, too.

Another cost is learning to become good stewards of all that God has given us. Some people believe that we must tithe, give 10% of our income to God. I am in that camp, but there is much to give beyond a set 10%. That's just the beginning. Being good stewards includes careful use and sharing of all that you are and all that you have. Our United Methodist rite of acceptance into our church membership asks, "Will you support the church with your prayers, presence, gifts and service?" That's a pretty good summation of stewardship.

Once we've considered the costs of repentance the last step is to decide to repent. We've thought about it, looking at the need for repentance, those places in our lives where we cry out for change. We've considered the cost of making such a change. We've been somewhat sobered by the thought of all that we will need to give up. And we've come to the point of deciding to repent. This is a critical point.

Many people can become convinced of sin in their lives and their need to repent. They may consider the costs of repentance, but they don't move to the finish line, so to speak; they remain stuck in the consideration mode. They don't make the decision to repent.

Seems like that's how it is with some of the important decisions we need to make in life, we put them off. We think about making the decision, but we don't do it.

If you are in the place of deciding to trust Jesus, to repent and follow Jesus, you need to decide to do it. Do it very soon. Do it today.

If you repented once years ago, guess what?

It's an ongoing activity. We who have been living with Jesus as our Lord for a long time need to keep our repentance up to date. Stuff has a way of accumulating and pulling us down if we are not keeping current with our forgiving and being forgiven.

John cried out in the desert—Prepare ye the way of the LORD. Prepare your hearts to see the salvation of God.

Luke 3: 7-18

7 So John said to the crowds that came out to be baptized by him, "You offspring of vipers! Who warned you to flee from the coming wrath?8 Therefore produce fruit that proves your repentance, and don't begin to say to yourselves, 'We have Abraham as our father.' For I tell you that God can raise up children for Abraham from these stones! 9 Even now the ax is laid at the root of the trees, and every tree that does not produce good fruit will be cut down and thrown into the fire."

10 So the crowds were asking him, "What then should we do?" 11 John answered them, "The person who has two tunics must share with the person who has none, and the person who has food must do

likewise."12 Tax collectors also came to be baptized, and they said to him, "Teacher, what should we do?" 13 He told them, "Collect no more than you are required to." 14 Then some soldiers also asked him,

"And as for us—what should we do?"

He told them, "Take money from no one by violence or by false accusation, and be content with your pay."

15 While the people were filled with anticipation and they all wondered whether perhaps John could be the Christ, 16 John answered them all, "I baptize you with water, but one more powerful than I am is coming—I am not worthy to untie the strap of his sandals. He will baptize you with the Holy Spirit and fire. 17 His winnowing fork is in his hand to clean out his threshing floor and to gather the wheat into his storehouse, but the chaff he will burn up with inextinguishable fire."

18 And in this way, with many other exhortations, John proclaimed good news to the people.

<u>POWER CONNECTION</u>

The Christmas season is so pretty and colorful.

Who would purposefully put those two strong colors—RED and GREEN—together. They don't complement one another. Yet we never think about it today, except to think—they're Christmas colors. It's hard to even remove that identity of Christmas colors from the mix of RED and GREEN.

The tree is wonderful, too. I wasn't here when it was dressed this year, but I can tell it took some time to decorate. It was painstaking work, carefully unpacking all the Chrismons and hanging them on the tree. There's one thing that's missing, though.

The tree is lifeless as it is. It needs to be connected to the power to really turn it on.

St. Luke's lesson today is about power, switching on the power of Christ in our lives.

The lesson begins with John the Baptists' ministry--how he called the people to repentance, to prepare them for the Christ who was coming.

John was quite a character; he was not your average man on the street. He lived out in the desert—camel's hair coat—honey and locusts to eat.

John told the people that he baptized them with water, but one was coming who would baptize with the Holy Spirit and with fire.

John's baptism was to prepare the people for

Christ's baptism. When Christ came he would give us the power to live our new lives of faith. This lesson brings up a question that I don't hear often addressed by the Church today. What sort of Baptism did I receive when I was baptized? Was it John's baptism or Christ's? Did I receive the Holy Spirit when I was baptized? How would I know?

John's Baptism came first. John came, preparing the way for the Christ.

His message told the people to repent and be baptized for the forgiveness of their sins. The words he used were very sobering. He called them a brood of vipers!

John asked them "who warned you to flee the wrath to come? (On the desert floor, where John was living, range fires came about spontaneously, and the critters would run from the holocaust around them, seeking safe ground.)

John called his listeners vipers—poisonous snakes--who would flee such a conflagration. He knew they needed to repent, how much they needed to flee their wicked ways.

The idea of repentance has, over the years, sometimes been confused with the idea of "being sorry" or properly contrite for our sins. But Christian repentance means to change one's mind. When John called the people to prepare for the Christ, he called them to change their minds from their normal, self- centered way of thinking and doing to change their minds, becoming what God had meant for them to be.

Repentance prepares us for Christ's coming. It humbles us; it cleans up our lives, and it calls us to refocus ourselves on our new life. Wouldn't it be nice to have the slate of our lives wiped clean? That is, wiped clean of all the errors of the past, all the hurts and wrongs that have been done to us, that we would have no pain associated with any such thing?

Wouldn't it be nice that every wrong we have done, be it big or small, would also be wiped away? It would no longer be an issue; we would have a whole new beginning. That would provide a whole new start in this world. There would be no reason to spend any energy or time on painful memories. There would be no self-condemnation, no remorse any longer.

That's what repentance is all about, wiping the slate clean. John's call to repentance was exactly that—wiping the slate clean in preparation for the one who would come fill their lives with new energy and power to live a new life.

John's baptism prepared the people for Christ's empowerment, the second step in the baptism.

St. Luke writes that when St. Paul was in Ephesus he met a group of new believers in Christ. After spending some time with them, Paul asked them if they had received the Holy Spirit when they came to believe? They replied that they hadn't even heard about the Holy Spirit or that there is a Holy Spirit. Paul asked them "Into what then were you baptized?" They answered, "Into John's baptism." (Acts 19)

Paul said, "John baptized with the baptism of repentance, telling the people to believe in the one who was to come after him, that is, in Jesus."

Paul recognized that these believers were still back in the preparation stage and that they needed the Holy Spirit to fill them. They were baptized in the name of the Lord Jesus. Then Paul laid his hands on each of them and prayed for the Holy Spirit to come fill them, and suddenly, they showed signs of the Holy Spirit's presence.

This scripture tells us that John's baptism for repentance and forgiveness of sins is not all there is. Christ's baptism sends the Holy Spirit into believers, to strengthen them, to give them power for the coming challenge of walking in their new life with Christ.

In the early church Christian baptism had two moments, or steps, making one unitary rite. The first moment was the water washing, when the new believer was dipped or poured on with water. The water washing was for the remission of sins; all the believer's sins, up to that point in their lives, were forgiven. Following this water washing, the newly baptized person was then anointed with oil, and a prayer for the Holy Spirit to come into his or her life was spoken.

So there were two moments—the moment of water and the moment of oil-- the water for the sins, and the oil for the Holy Spirit, the power.

The early church always included the Holy Spirit

in their baptisms, but a funny thing happened as the church began to grow. In 313 A.D. church growth magnified tremendously almost overnight. Emperor Constantine declared that the church was now free to meet in the open, making the Christian religion a legal organization.

Christians were free to build churches, hold meetings and gather members. Many, many people came to join the Church, and they needed to be baptized. At this point the Church was spread all over the Roman world, all the area around the Mediterranean Sea. Each big city had a bishop who was the superintendent for the Church in that location. It was the bishop's job to pray over the oil before it was used for the prayer for the Holy Spirit.

The bishop couldn't be at every little church in every village when baptisms took place, so the Bishop of Rome suggested that the first moment of the Baptism be done--the water washing for the forgiveness of sins. Then, as the bishop could arrange his schedule, he would come around to the different communities and confirm these new members. This visiting by the bishop might happen years after the baptism occurred. (That is actually the history of where confirmation came from, which we still observe today.)

I believe that the power of the Holy Spirit is not always recognized in our lives today. There are some people who say that they don't believe in God. They somehow manage to miss the world full of indications of God's creative work in this world.

St. Paul said those people are without excuse, after all, they can see God's handiwork every day in this world. In the same way, he Holy Spirit is sometimes missed in our Christian lives. People don't realize that the Holy Spirit is there available to us, ready to give us what we need. You might ask yourselves these questions, to see if the Holy Spirit is working in your life today

> Are you convinced that the Holy Spirit is at work in your life?

> Are you absolutely sure that He dwells in you and guides you?

> Has the Holy Spirit spoken to your own spirit and confirmed in you that you are a child of God?

> Are you aware of the Holy Spirit's presence in your life encouraging you to love God and your neighbor?

> Encouraging you to seek time alone with God each day?

> Encouraging you to seek forgiveness and to give it?

> Encouraging you to give freely of your time, your talents, your gifts and your service?

> Encouraging you to speak in kindness to one another?

> Encouraging you to remember all that Jesus taught and did?

Encouraging you to share your faith with others?

Do you feel the deep joy that the Holy Spirit gives?

We cannot live the life that God wants us to live, to be the people that God has called us to be without help from the Holy Spirit. But with the Holy Spirit working within us we will have power, wisdom, and strength to do just that.

Alone we cannot succeed, but God does not want us to fail. God has provided the Holy Spirit to us to help us along the way. It is part of God's plan for our lives that we have the Holy Spirit in our lives.

When Jesus said, "*And, Lo, I will be with you always.*" He meant that he would give us the Holy Spirit to be his presence always. The Holy Spirit comes into our lives when we ask him in. He is faithful to answer our prayers and to come fill us. For the Holy Spirit to be effective in our lives we need to trust that he is there for us.

After the disciples had been through everything with Jesus -- walking with him, hearing him preach, seeing him heal the sick, seeing him during the mounting tensions of the last week, his being arrested and tried and crucified and THEN rising again!

When they had done all that they still did not move out to spread the gospel. They didn't go out until they were filled with the Holy Spirit on Pentecost.

It was the Holy Spirit's dwelling in the disciples that gave them the vision, the courage, the strength, and the wisdom to follow Jesus' commission—"*Go, ye into all the world and make disciples.*" Before they had the Holy Spirit in them, they lacked the power to move.

Today, we can have the Holy Spirit in us. Jesus said that God is gracious to give us whatever we ask, especially the Holy Spirit. Remember Jesus' words?

> *If you then, who are evil, know how to give good gifts to your children, how much more will the heavenly Father give the Holy Spirit to those who ask him!"*

If we have repented our sins and have turned away from evil, then we are prepared for Christ's coming into our lives. It would be strange to have someone, all prepared for Christian life, but with no power to enable him/her to move. Like the Christmas tree here, when it was completely trimmed and ready to be our tree, how sad it would be not to connect it to the power and let it shine for all to see.

We need this power in our lives. When we repent we have begun to make preparations for our new life in Christ. Like the Christmas tree, which needs the lights to be switched on, we need to be connected to the power to light up our lives.

So, in like manner, we need to be connected to the power God's power in the Holy Spirit, so we can let our lights shine before the world, so that the world can see our lights and glorify God who is in Heaven!

Luke 3:21-22

21 Now when all the people were baptized, Jesus also was baptized. And while he was praying, the heavens opened, 22 and the Holy Spirit descended on him in bodily form like a dove. And a voice came from heaven, "You are my one dear Son; in you I take great delight."

REMEMBERING YOUR NAME

I understand that in Oriental society the family name is treasured and great measures are taken to insure its reputation. I've often heard that is how Chinese families get their children to excel so well in school, because they are told that they are responsible for carrying on the family name and helping it maintain its good reputation.

Our names carry with it some important information about us. Your name may tell the world that you belong to a certain family, which would put you in a category of one kind or another. You might be related to a family that owns much or one that has some celebrity in it. Your name goes hand in hand with your reputation. If you are respected and liked in the community your good name will carry you far.

On the other hand, if your reputation has become blemished, your name will precede you to places. A blemished name could be a serious source of trouble for you.

When we have children we may spend time trying to figure just the right name for the new little one. These days, since the gender of a child is often known ahead of time, science may have relieved the task a bit by eliminating one set of names from the list. If you know the child will be a boy, then boys' names only are necessary for to consider.

Our scripture today speaks of God calling Jesus by a new name.

Luke writes, *"After all the people were baptized, Jesus came to be baptized, and as he was praying, the heavens opened and the Holy Spirit descended on him in bodily form like a dove, and a voice came saying, 'You are my son, my beloved, in you I am well pleased.'"*

With those words, God was claiming Jesus, affirming who Jesus was, and indicting what his life and ministry would be.

What names are we known by? Do we have names that really reflect who we are? Are there some names that we wish we didn't have? Do you know that at your baptism we received a new name? That God gave each of us a new name at our baptism?

Jesus came to be baptized. Our text in Luke doesn't give any details on the actual baptism, but Luke does tell us that when all the people were baptized, and when Jesus also had been baptized and was praying, the heaven was opened, *22and the Holy Spirit descended upon him in bodily form like a dove. And a voice came from heaven, "You are my Son, the Beloved, with you I am well pleased."*

Jesus' baptism was the step he took as he initiated his active ministry. This moment of baptism marked the ending of his life as a private person and provided him with three important keys to his ministry. These were focus, connection to power, and affirmation.

We know that John's baptism was for repentance and forgiveness of sins, preparing people for the coming Messiah. Why, then did Jesus come, himself, to be baptized? He never sinned; he didn't need forgiveness.

Jesus' focus was on people, people who did need to repent and be forgiven. Jesus came to be counted as one with the people, to stand with them, and be known as one of them. God was at work here, with John at the Jordan. God was very active moving in people's hearts as they heard the prophet calling to them to seek God, repent and be forgiven.

Here was the place where God was active. That would be the best place for Jesus to begin his own ministry. Jesus came to the waters of baptism to be counted among the humans who were seeking God in their lives. Jesus' focus was on people and being one with them, speaking to them, reaching out to them, healing them and saving them.

Jesus was filled with God's Holy Spirit, connecting him to the power of God.

Luke says that as Jesus was praying, the heavens opened up and the Holy Spirit, in the form of a dove, swooped down and lighted on Jesus. Jesus was filled with God's Holy Spirit fro that moment on. The Holy Spirit was present and engaged with Jesus from the very start.

Scripture tells us that Mary conceived the child by the Holy Spirit; it came upon her. The Holy Spirit was very much part of Jesus' from the outset, but at the moment of baptism, it was apparent even to the public view, as the Spirit appeared to come upon Jesus in the form of a dove.

You may remember my illustration about the importance of our being connected to the power of God in order to walk our Christian walk. The Holy Spirit will come to fill us when we have made ourselves ready for Him through repentance and accepting forgiveness.

Then a voice was heard from heaven. (St. Luke suggests that the voice was directed to Jesus and was, perhaps, heard only by him.) The voice said, *"You are my son, the beloved; in you I am well pleased."*

God gave Jesus words of affirmation, telling him that they were in relationship—father and son-- and that what Jesus had done and was about to do was pleasing to God.

Scholars will tell us that these words actually come from two Hebrew Bible passages and they reveal much about Jesus' upcoming ministry. The first part, "You are my son", comes from Ps. 2:7. It is part of an enthronement hymn, to bring in a new king from David's line.

Do you remember God's promise to King David, which we read in 2 Samuel 7:14? God promised that a king would come from David's line who would rule forever in an eternal kingdom. Jesus is the son God is talking about, he one who would rule forever.

The voice continued saying, "In you I a well pleased." Again, these words come as an echo from Hebrew Bible. In Isaiah 42:1 those words are found. They come from the beginning of Isaiah's prophecy about the suffering servant. Let me read a few verses for you:

> *7 6 I am the LORD, I have called you in righteousness, I have taken you by the hand and kept you; I have given you as a covenant to the*

people, a light to the nations,

8 to open the eyes that are blind, to bring out the prisoners from the dungeon, from the prison those who sit in darkness.

9 I am the LORD, that is my name; my glory I give to no other,

10   nor my praise to idols.

11   See, the former things have come to pass, and new things I now declare;

12   before they spring forth, I tell you of them.

This verse in Isaiah continues on to Chapter 53, which clearly prophesies about how the suffering servant shall live and die.

Isaiah 53

13   3He was despised and rejected by others; a man of suffering and acquainted with infirmity;

14   4Surely he has borne our infirmities and carried our diseases;

15But he was wounded for our transgressions, upon him was the punishment that made us whole, and by his bruises we are healed. and the LORD has laid on him the iniquity of us all. because he poured out himself to death, and was numbered with the transgressors; yet he bore the sin of many, and made intercession for the transgressors.

In those few words (you are my beloved Son, in you I am well pleased) God, the Father, gave his son the affirmation he needed to begin his ministry. To know that God recognized him as His Son and to know the direction his ministry would follow. Jesus knew right from the beginning of his ministry how it would end. He knew the prophecy well.

Christians are baptized people. (If you have not been baptized, but have come to faith in Christ, your first response to him is to be baptized in obedience to his command that all disciples are baptized.)

At the time of your baptism you, too, were given a new name. Like Jesus, who heard the voice saying, "You are my beloved son," We, too are called in a new way from the moment of our own baptism.

We are called Christian. We will forever be known as a follower of Jesus Christ. By that new name we are also known as a child of God.

Remember in the prolog to John's Gospel, he writes:

15   *"to all who received [Jesus as Christ], who believed in his name, he gave power to become children of God,*

16   *We are called the children of*

God when we believe and are baptized.

Like Jesus, who was told by his father that he was God's child at his baptism, we, too can be a member of the family of God. That makes a tremendous difference in our lives.

Being a child of God means we belong to God.

God through Christ heals us, forgives us, provides new life to us, and promises us eternal life.

Our new relationship to God also gives us a mission to do. We are to live as the people of God, giving God glory in every way we can.

I'd like you to play a little game with me. You can find a half-sized sheet of paper in your bulletin. You'll notice that the paper has a straight line across it. On the line I'd like you to mark off little sections that will represent a certain time span in your life, maybe five or ten years. I want you to note on the paper the year you were baptized. You might even write your name as it was given you then. Then I'd like you to put little marks on your page according to your graph, indicating moments in your life when important things happened. (This graph never has to be shown to anyone else. It is for you.) You might indicate when you got out of school, when you got married, when children came. Be sure to note the date, if you know it, when you knew for sure that you believed, that you trusted Jesus for your life. Also pinpoint any moments that were moments of spiritual connection, times when you felt God was present in your life. I also hope you pin point any times of trouble, times when you fell or hurt or knew you had sinned.

Now I want you to ask yourselves a question about those times. Actually, you'll need to take more time on this, so this can only be a beginning for you. But during those times that you pin point on your paper, I want you to think in each case, "Because of my baptism, I have been called a child of God.

What difference did that make in this instance?" Did I remember at the time that I was a child of God? Did remembering that make a difference in how I reacted?

It may be that in some cases you forgot you were a child of God. And at other times you remembered and took some steps that others would not have taken.

You might find yourself saying, "because of my baptism I did such and such or chose such and such or moved to some place new.

You might hear yourself saying, "I know that God was with me in that situation.

> I survived.

> I was healed.

> I was led in a new direction.

> I met someone who became important to me.

Baptism only happens once in a person's life.

Once is all that is necessary for anyone, but we can celebrate our baptism, the time God welcomed us into God's family, when we celebrate the LORD's Supper.

These days we United Methodists celebrate the Lord's Supper monthly, although, we certainly could celebrate it every time we gather. When we celebrate the Eucharist, we are reaffirming our belief in Christ and asking for our sins to be forgiven. We are celebrating the wonderful work God has done for us in Jesus Christ, providing new life and eternal life in him.

Luke 4: 4-30

⁴ *Jesus answered, "It is written: 'Man shall not live on bread alone.'[a] "*

⁵ *The devil led him up to a high place and showed him in an instant all the kingdoms of the world. ⁶ And he said to him, "I will give you all their authority and splendor; it has been given to me, and I can give it to anyone I want to. ⁷ If you worship me, it will all be yours."*

⁸ *Jesus answered, "It is written: 'Worship the Lord your God and serve him only.'[b] "*

⁹ *The devil led him to Jerusalem and had him stand on the highest point of the temple. "If you are the Son of God," he said, "throw yourself down from here. ¹⁰ For it is written:*

"'He will command his angels concerning you to guard you carefully;

¹¹ *they will lift you up in their hands, so that you will not strike your foot against a stone.'[c]"*

¹² *Jesus answered, "It is said: 'Do not put the Lord your God to the test.'[d] "*

¹³ When the devil had finished all this tempting, he left him until an opportune time.

¹⁴ Jesus returned to Galilee in the power of the Spirit, and news about him spread through the whole countryside. ¹⁵ He was teaching in their synagogues, and everyone praised him.

¹⁶ He went to Nazareth, where he had been brought up, and on the Sabbath day he went into the synagogue, as was his custom. He stood up to read, ¹⁷ and the scroll of the prophet Isaiah was handed to him.

Unrolling it, he found the place where it is written:

¹⁸ "The Spirit of the Lord is on me, because he has anointed me to proclaim good news to the poor.

He has sent me to proclaim freedom for the prisoners and recovery of sight for the blind, to set the oppressed free,

¹⁹ to proclaim the year of the Lord's favor." [e]

²⁰ Then he rolled up the scroll, gave it back to the attendant and sat down. The eyes of everyone in the synagogue were fastened

on him.²¹ He began by saying to them, "Today this scripture is fulfilled in your hearing."

²² All spoke well of him and were amazed at the gracious words that came from his lips. "Isn't this Joseph's son?" they asked.

²³ Jesus said to them, "Surely you will quote this proverb to me: 'Physician, heal yourself!' And you will tell me, 'Do here in your hometown what we have heard that you did in Capernaum.'"

²⁴ "Truly I tell you," he continued, "no prophet is accepted in his hometown. ²⁵ I assure you that there were many widows in Israel in Elijah's time, when the sky was shut for three and a half years and there was a severe famine throughout the land. ²⁶ Yet Elijah was not sent to any of them, but to a widow in Zarephath in the region of Sidon. ²⁷ And there were many in Israel with leprosy⁽ⁱ⁾ in the time of Elisha the prophet, yet not one of them was cleansed— only Naaman the Syrian."

²⁸ All the people in the synagogue were furious when they heard this.²⁹ They got up, drove him out of the town,

and took him to the brow of the hill on which the town was built, in order to throw him off the cliff.[30] But he walked right through the crowd and went on his way.

INAUGURATION DAY?

Today we have a new president in our country. He may even be worshiping in a United Methodist Church in Washington, D.C. As I understand he is a UM. George W. was inaugurated into office of president yesterday. He has been duly sworn in, pledging his oath of loyalty to the United States and to our U.S. Constitution. Mr. Bush then gave an inaugural speech in which he spoke of his vision for his work and for us, the American people. He gave us many good challenges. Yesterday was a big day for the new administration. They partied to all hours of last night. They will have a big job in front of them in these next four years.

Our lesson today has a sort of parallel to the current inaugural events. St. Luke writes that Jesus announced to the people in the synagogue that he is the Christ, the one anointed to bring in the Kingdom of God. He used the words from the prophet Isaiah to clarify his mission —to proclaim release to the captives, give sight to the blind, to bind up the brokenhearted and to proclaim the acceptable year of the Lord's favor.

I don't know if you personally think that the inauguration of President Bush is good news or not. I expect there may be varying opinions here this morning what Mr. Bush needs our prayers and God's grace.

It is definitely good news, though, that Jesus was anointed to be the Christ, for his whole purpose in life was to bring the Kingdom of God into this world.

Last week we learned that Jesus often used

something old and gave it a new meaning. Here, again, we can see Jesus reaching into Hebrew Bible to words written by the prophet Isaiah and applying them to this new day.

Jesus took the old prophecy and made it central to his new work. This scene in the synagogue in Nazareth could be considered Jesus' inaugural moment, when he claimed the title of the anointed One, the Messiah, and spoke of his mission through the words of Isaiah. It tells who Jesus was and what he was about.

This morning we shall visit the prophecy of Isaiah briefly to see how those words spoke first to the exiles in Babylon, and then we shall turn to see how Jesus used them to focus on his own ministry, how Isaiah's words beautifully described Jesus' identity and his purpose, the inauguration of God's Kingdom on earth.

Isaiah lived in the time of the Babylonian conquest, about 600 years before Christ. During that time a great many of the Jews living in Jerusalem, the nobility, the upper classes, were all taken captive by the Babylonians. They were dragged from their homes and their lives and taken off to Babylon

This was a terrible time for the Jews. They had lost greatly and were deeply depressed.

God told Isaiah to write to these exiles.

Isaiah may even have been referring to himself, as the one anointed to preach the good news to the oppressed and to proclaim release to the captives.

Today's scripture in Luke follows Jesus' baptism and temptations. Luke moves from the temptation with just two short verses, 14 and 15, where Luke summarizes Jesus' early ministry in Galilee.

He wrote: "*14Then Jesus, filled with the power of the Spirit, returned to Galilee, and a report about him spread through all the surrounding country. 15He began to teach in their synagogues and was praised by everyone.*"

So Jesus had acquired quite a reputation and a following. Reports about him were everywhere. People buzzed about what they had heard about the young, wandering teacher, Jesus. He was highly praised by all.

Then Luke focuses on Jesus' hometown of Nazareth. Luke tells us that Jesus went to the synagogue on the Sabbath day as was his custom.

We might remember that Jesus never failed in any of the Jewish laws. Jesus always attended the synagogue services on the Sabbath. The synagogue was the local house of worship for the Jews.

The service at the synagogue included the Shema, that is: Hear, O Israel: The LORD our God is one LORD: And thou shalt love the LORD thy God with all Thine heart, and with all thy soul, and with all thy might.

There would be prayers, readings from the Law and the Prophets of the Hebrew Bible, a sermon, and 18 benedictions.

That would have been the sort of service that Jesus attended in the synagogue in Nazareth on that day.

Luke writes that Jesus stood and read from a scroll that was handed to him by the attendant. That was the position of adult males in the community, to take a turn at reading from the Holy Writings.

Then following the reading, the reader would translate the words and maybe make a comment on them, to help the listeners understand better.

(We read something about that in our OT lesson this morning when Nehemiah read from the scrolls and then translated them for the people.

The scroll that Jesus was given was the book of Isaiah the prophet.

Jesus took the scroll and unrolled it to the portion we know as chapter 61: 1-2. He read:

18   *"The Spirit of the Lord is upon me, because he has anointed me to bring good news to the poor.*

He has sent me to proclaim release to the captives and recovery of sight to the blind, to let the oppressed go free,

19   *to proclaim the year of the Lord's favor."*

Luke reports that every eye in the room was fixed on Jesus. They were glued to their seats, watching, ready.

Then Jesus sat down and began to speak. (Remember when Jesus sat down, he was taking the position of a teacher.) He was known in the land as being a teacher, his reputation had spread quickly that he had become a teacher.

Then Jesus spoke saying, *"This day the scripture has been fulfilled in your hearing."*

The congregation had heard the Isaiah verse before.

They were actually looking forward to the coming of the anointed one that Isaiah spoke of. That prophecy was a dream among the Jews, but to hear this young man, this fellow who had grown up among them, saying that this scripture had come true that very day, that they were witnesses to it. How extraordinary! How could that be?

When Jesus received the scroll, he knew exactly what verse he would read for the people that day. That verse encapsulated the very ministry he was about. And it pointed to the anointed one, the one chosen by God to bring about God's kingdom.

We need to remember that the Hebrew word for anointed one is Messiah. That word translates into the Greek as Christos. So, we call Jesus the Messiah or the Christ.

When Jesus opened that Isaiah scripture and then told the people *"Today this scripture has been fulfilled in your hearing,"* Jesus was identifying himself as the Messiah, the Christ, the anointed one!

You've heard it said before that Jesus, the Christ, is foretold in the Hebrew writings in many places. It was Jesus who pointed us to that fact. He told the people that Sabbath Day that he was the Christ, the expected one, the one God promised. He pointed to that scripture.

At the end of Luke in chapter 24, where the two disciples are walking down from Jerusalem to the little town of Emmaus, they met the risen Lord on the road. In their conversation that day, Jesus also pointed to the prophecies,   especially in Isaiah, about the suffering servant, as telling of himself.

When Jesus read from the Scriptures that day in

Nazareth and announced that this reading had come true that morning, as all were watching on, Jesus was telling the people that something brand new was happening, and that he was integrally connected with its coming about

We have been entertained recently by seeing all the falderal and trappings that have accompanied our new president into office. We've had days of reports and commentaries on every aspect of the Bush inaugural balls and office taking. There was plenty of hoopla and extravagance. Bush is the president. He has many duties in his office and much that he wants to accomplish. But first he is the leader of our country, even the leader of the free world.

Jesus had a purpose, the Isaiah scripture spoke of that purpose, but first it spoke of who would fill that purpose, the anointed one. Jesus is that person, the Christ, the Messiah, the King.

That morning in the synagogue Jesus told the congregation that God had anointed him Christ; his anointing had occurred following Jesus' baptism when the Holy Spirit descended on him like a dove. Jesus claimed the title of Christ for himself. That is the "who" of this lesson. Jesus is the Christ.

This is an intriguing piece here, because there are several occasions in Luke when we hear Jesus caution someone not to share this information about his identity with others.

There were several demon-possessed people who would cry out that Jesus was the Christ, the Son of God. And when Peter named Jesus to be the Christ of God, Jesus cautioned Peter and the others to tell no one of this matter.

This synagogue event took place rather late in Jesus' ministry. Although it appears in chapter four, early in the Gospel, Luke was not actually trying for a straight, chronological telling of Jesus' ministry. Rather, Luke wanted to bring forward early this prophecy, because it spoke of Jesus' purpose and identity. Jesus was anointed by God to bring healing to the people in two ways—

He would bring healing to their physical world and to their eternal lives. Listen to Isaiah's words about Jesus' purpose:

The Messiah would bring good news to the poor; proclaim release to the captives and recovery of sight to the blind. He would let the oppressed go free, and proclaim the favorable year of the Lord.

Jesus' purpose was two-fold: to bring healing to the physical world and to proclaim, in fact to bring in, the Kingdom of God.

We must never forget that Jesus brings healing in this world first. Jesus touched lives in many ways— he restored the sick, the lame, the blind. He gave them new lives as he restored their physical lives. Jesus also touched and healed the inner lives of people. There were those who were dejected, oppressed, demon-possessed, bruised from this world. He also brought healing to them.

Jesus renewed the lives of those who were caught in sin. He forgave them and put them on the road to new life, too. Jesus was very much a healer of the physical and emotional ills of this world. He continues to be that today.

And finally, Jesus' purpose was to proclaim the favorable year of the LORD. That is, he came to announce the Kingdom of God. That it was at hand; it was there for them. This was the second healing that Jesus brought.

Jesus taught that the Kingdom of God was here on earth, available to all who would follow him. The Kingdom of God also leads mortals into life eternal with God. Our faith in Christ will make the initial step into God's kingdom now in this world, but it continues through eternity.

Jesus made a very simple statement to the congregation that day. He said the prophecy had been fulfilled. But Jesus' meaning was not simple; it was of great importance.

You may remember in Matthew's Gospel that John the Baptist, who was in the dungeon in King Herod's palace, sent two of his disciples to Jesus with the question, *"Are you the One who is to come, or are we to wait for another?*

Jesus answered John's disciples with nearly the same words as he read from the Isaiah scroll in this morning's reading:

"Go and tell John what you hear and see: the blind receive their sight, the lame walk, the lepers are cleansed, the deaf hear, the dead are raised, and the poor have good news brought to them. (Matt 11:4-5.)

There, again, we see Jesus announcing who he is and what his purpose is: To bring healing to the people and to bring the good news of God's eternal kingdom to all who will come.

Behold what love God has for us! God loves us so very much that he sent his son to bring healing to our lives today and life eternal for us tomorrow. Amen.

Luke 5: 1-11

8 When Simon Peter saw this, he fell at Jesus' knees and said, "Go away from me, Lord; I am a sinful man!" 9 For he and all his companions were astonished at the catch of fish they had taken, 10 and so were James and John, the sons of Zebedee, Simon's partners.

Then Jesus said to Simon, "Don't be afraid; from now on you will fish for people." 11 So they pulled their boats up on shore, left everything and followed him.

THE CALL

We went to the Top of the River not long ago, and Buddy pointed out to me a picture of a man holding a fish that is as big as he is, but Buddy laughed and said that the picture was a trick. The fish picture had been enlarged to the size of the man and then put back in the picture. I'd love to hear the story that man tells about the big fish he caught.

I'm not a fisherman—or a fisherwoman. I have been fishing on a lake when I was young. I think I may even have had some nibbles and even a couple of catches, but I can't really call myself a fisherperson.

Today's story, though, is about fishermen, good fishermen, men who made their living fishing in the lake.

Simon thought he knew himself quite well. He was a fisherman. He knew about fishing. He had grown up by the sea, actually the lake. He was good at fishing. He and his brother Andrew were together in business, along with their friends, maybe even cousins, Zebedee and his two sons, James and John. Each family had their own boat and rigging and all that goes with fishing. They had spent untold hours every week at fishing, since they were young men.

Now they were adults. Simon married, but his wife had died. He still took Sabbath meals at the home of his mother-in-law. She was a good cook. Simon supplied the fish, of course.

The fishing business was not just time on the water. It was that, but it was also cleaning the boat and the nets after each expedition. It was also about cleaning the fish and preparing them for market. The men occasionally even took salted fish to the big city of Jerusalem. That was quite an event when they went there. They saw more of the world on those occasions.

Simon knew that he was good at fishing; he was a leader in the community. By his sheer stature people looked up to him. He also had a voice that carried well. Oh yes, Simon could be heard quite well.

Simon also knew, if he really thought about it, that he was not the best man. He could curse with the best of men. His thoughts were not always pure. His tongue could get him into big trouble, sometimes. But Simon did try to observe the laws of the Jews. He at least tried to follow them.

Then one day something new happened. Simon heard about a man who was new to the district. He was a wandering preacher, a man a bit younger than Simon, but one that many people were talking about. Simon determined to find him.

Andrew and Simon went together. Perhaps they listened to the man called Jesus several times, and then one night Simon invited Jesus over for dinner—at his mother-in-law's house. But, would you believe? His mother-in-law was down with the flu, and she was in no mood to serve Simon and his guests.

But Jesus stepped into the house, went to the woman's bedside, spoke to her, and the fever lifted. She rose and began serving them.

A couple of days later, Simon and Andrew and the Zebedees had fished all night long. It was one of those nights that wore on and on, but there were no fish to be had. Finally, after a day break, the came back on shore and began cleaning up.

As they sat at their nets, a crowd of people came along. They were following Jesus, the preacher, hanging on his every word. When Jesus saw Simon he called to him to put his boat back on the water, so that he could speak from it. That would keep the crowds at a distance, allowing them to hear him, but preventing his being overtaken by them.

Simon did as Jesus asked, and he went back to work.

Jesus spoke a bit longer, then he looked at Simon and his comrades and said, *"Take your boat out into the deep water and let out your nets."*

'What! Did Jesus not see that they were cleaning their nets? Did he not realize that they had already been out fishing?' Simon spoke up, *"Lord, we've worked all night through, but to no avail ... but if you say so, we'll try again."*

Simon and Andrew got into the boat, along with Jesus, and pushed out for deep water. When they got to a certain place, Jesus told them the let out their nets. They did.

Would you believe? The fish came running for the nets! They came and came and came! Simon was too far out on the water to be heard, but he motioned to his fellow fishermen on the shore to come, bring their boat and nets and help them.

Before long both boats were filling up with the enormous catch of fish! There were so many fish that the boats were in danger of actually sinking!

Simon stopped. He had been so busy hauling in fish and exclaiming to everyone, "Look! Look at those fish! I've never in all my born days seen so many fish in one place!"

Then Simon stopped and thought. He was in the midst of a miracle. This Jesus was not just some old preacher he was far more than that. He had special knowledge and power that Simon had never seen.

Simon was humbled by the comparison. Here he was a dirty, smelly old fisherman, and in his boat stood a man who commanded the very life in the seas to come.

He fell to Jesus' feet. (I can just see Simon sinking to his knees among all the fish on the floor of the boat.) "*Master, he said, 'depart from me, a sinner.'*

But Jesus replied, *'Fear not, from now on you will be fishing for men."*

Before that moment, Simon knew who he was; he was a fisherman. Now everything had changed.

I believe that's the way it is for each of us,
when we come into the presence of Jesus.
We are changed when we meet Jesus.

When I was a young woman, just about Mary
Beth's age, my life was yet ahead of me. I was
a fairly good student; I enjoyed music and
church, especially the MYF. I never missed a
Sunday at church.

That summer our youth choir was asked to sing
at the Annual Conference, which is held each
year at Redlands University. About 80 of us
piled on the bus and took off for Southern
California.

That day as we sat on the bleachers of the
football stadium, the Bishop preached
about our following Jesus, that Jesus was
calling us to be in full-time Christian
ministry.

I heard those words. I knew he was speaking
the truth. There were many in my family who
had been in full-time Christian work before me.
There were plenty of examples for me to
follow. But I hadn't thought about what I
wanted to do, and I think I didn't want it
decided for me before I had given it any
thought. I really didn't want to respond. I fought
within myself when I heard those words of
invitation, "Come down here and give your life
to Jesus. Come down and sign up for full-time
Christian service."

I knew on the one hand that I should do it, I
should go. Several of my good friends were
listening to that same voice and were getting
up and moving down the bleachers to the field

where the Bishop was. I saw them get up. Something inside me told me I needed to go, and something inside me told me, "No, I don't know what it is I'd like to do. I'd like to wait and think about it."

The music kept playing. I couldn't avoid the sounds in my head, "Marjie, you need to do this. It is for you." Finally, I did get up and make that trip. I signed up, just as the Bishop had asked.

This picture of Simon falling at Jesus' feet and calling himself a sinner, has an echo in the Hebrew Bible. Back in the book of Isaiah, when the prophet Isaiah first got his call from God, Isaiah tells that he had the same reaction as did Simon on the boat.

For Isaiah, though, he was in the Temple in Jerusalem. As he stood there in the Temple he had a great vision of God. It must have been overwhelming, just in its size. Isaiah says that the Lord was sitting on a throne, and that the hem of his robe filled the Temple! The hem of his robe! That would make this a very, very large person! Isaiah also saw angels around the Lord, with many wings—covering their face and body, and flying.

When Isaiah saw this vision he cried out, "Woe is me! I am lost. I am a man of unclean lips, and I live in a world of unclean lips. Yet I have seen the Lord!". Then the Lord asked, "Whom can we send and who will go for us? And Isaiah replied, "Here I am, Lord, Send Me."

I'd like to share a picture of following that really fits nicely here. I tried to get it as a movie clip, but it wasn't to be.

Perhaps some of you are fans of the T.V. show, The West Wing. There was a little incident that was on at the beginning of the second year that I happened to see last week, and thought, isn't that the perfect picture of someone dropping everything and following?

There were two young men, Josh and Sam. They must have known one another back in school and were good friends. We are to understand that they both have the great altruistic ideals of young men and are beginning their own careers, wanting to do the right thing, but not knowing exactly where to find it.

One day Josh has been told about another man, an older man, a statesman, who might be running for president. Josh is challenged to go to New Hampshire and hear him to see for himself if this man isn't the right one to follow.

Before Josh goes, however, he finds his old friend Sam and tells him about this older man. Josh wants Sam to go with him to hear him. But Sam puts Josh off. He says, "If he's the right one, you let me know."

A bit later Sam is in a big business meeting with lots of high-powered attorneys and businessmen, when Josh appears at the window looking into the room where Sam is. Sam is distracted by Josh's presence. In fact, Josh has a great gleam on his face. He never says a word, but you can read his pleasure on his face. Sam tries to listen to the businessmen for a bit, and finally right in the middle of someone talking to him, Sam gets up and leaves the room. Someone asks Sam where he is going, leaving them right in the middle of the meeting, and he says, "New Hampshire, I'm going to New Hampshire." That was where the candidate would be found. He left everything and followed.

St. Paul tells us that that day the fishermen left their nets and boats and followed Jesus. We can spend a lifetime seeing God all around us, and perhaps ignore those marvelous indicators, but when God speaks to us personally, that's another matter.

We can be overwhelmed by a gorgeous sunset, or a big, double rainbow, or the birth a of new child. Those are wonderful examples of God's work in our world, but they may not be personal. (The birth of a baby would be.)

When we realize that God is here and we're in God's presence, then we can be over-awed with thrill, but there's lots more to it than that.

Simon was overawed, he fell on his knees and cried to the Lord—"*Depart from me, I am a sinner.*" But, of course, Jesus didn't depart. He had a plan for Simon. Jesus told Simon that he would be fishing for men, now. He had a new job with Jesus, fishing for men.

Isn't that what happens to each of us? When we find God is in our lives, we also learn that we, too, have a new job, something that Jesus has in mind for us to do.

Luke 6: 17-26

17 He went down with them and stood on a level place. A large crowd of his disciples was there and a great number of people from all over Judea, from Jerusalem, and from the coastal region around Tyre and Sidon, 18 who had come to hear him and to be healed of their diseases. Those troubled by impure spirits were cured, 19 and the people all tried to touch him, because power was coming from him and healing them all.

20 Looking at his disciples, he said:

"Blessed are you who are poor,
  for yours is the kingdom of God.
21 Blessed are you who hunger
  now, for you will be satisfied.
Blessed are you who weep
  now, for you will laugh.
22 Blessed are you when people hate
  you, when they exclude you and
  insult you and reject your name as
  evil,
  because of the Son of Man.

23 "Rejoice in that day and leap for joy, because great is your reward in heaven. For that is how their ancestors treated the prophets.

24 "But woe to you who are rich,
    for you have already received your comfort.
25 Woe to you who are well fed
    now, for you will go hungry.
Woe to you who laugh now,
    for you will mourn and weep.
26 Woe to you when everyone speaks well of you,
    for that is how their ancestors treated the false prophets.

UNEASY LOVE

"Agape is a willingness to go to any length to restore community." (Dr. Martin Luther King, Jr)

I suppose that even little people can tell us about love. Didn't we just celebrate St. Valentine's Day last week? Love is about giving little hearts to people we love. Love is about receiving cards and messages from those who love us. Love is the warm feeling we have when we are near someone who is special to us. Love can be for friends, like brotherly and sisterly love; love can be for families; and, yes, there is that special someone, who has taken our heart--our Valentine. Love is a great subject; where would we be without love?

Our lesson this morning is about love. We read that Jesus spoke to his disciples about love, but his words sound like commands:

Jesus said, "Love your enemies, do good to those who hate you, bless those who curse you, pray for those who abuse you."

Then he went on to talk about the way sinners love— they love the lovable, There's nothing difficult about loving someone who is friendly, smiley, fun to be with.

Even sinners love those who will return their love. But Jesus told his disciples to love their enemies … to give when they can't expect repayment, to lend without expecting return.

It's easy to love when love is returned. Easy

love is fun. I think we thrive on it, but the kind of love that Jesus is talking about with the disciples is not easy. It requires a lot from us. It requires that we put away our pride and ask forgiveness, or give forgiveness, or understanding, or help when it's inconvenient.

It asks us to go the second mile, when it's definitely not convenient. This "uneasy love" pinches us and forces us to live outside our comfort zone.

Uneasy love is a challenge to each of us.

I call this love that Jesus commanded "Uneasy Love", because this kind of love is not obvious or easy to live. Uneasy love" can be summed up by saying it is the willingness of a person to go to any length to restore community. (I want to give Brother Martin Luther King, Jr. credit for this definition.)

This morning we shall begin by thinking about this "uneasy love" and consider the why and how of this love—why this love is necessary and how it can be done. I want us to remember that "Uneasy Love" is doing whatever it takes to restore community.

Uneasy love is my term. The word for this love in Greek is Agape, or Divine love, love that comes from God.

Jesus tells us to love our enemies, that means we need to love those who are not loving to us, who are unlovable, or those with whom we have a problem.

It really doesn't matter where the enemy comes

from—whether we decided that someone or some group is now our enemy or if that designation came from the other party, naming us as the enemy. Either way, the relationship is there, and at that point there is room, in fact need, to address this enemy with love. Suddenly we have an object of "uneasy love" for us to deal with.

Why should we love our enemies? Uneasy love seems to go against basic logic. It flies in the face of the norm.

That's not how society works. An enemy is someone for whom you do not have good will.

Jesus wants more from us as disciples than what the norm in society expects. He described how it is no big accomplishment to love those who love us. He said even sinners love those who love them. And sinners do good for those who do good for them. And sinners lend to others when they know that whatever they lend will be returned.

The normal love, which everyone understands, is simplistic— you love me and I'll love you back. It is childish love, the kind that receives first and then reciprocates.

We all start with that sort of love,

Jesus was telling his disciples, they are not just ordinary people, as disciples they have been called to follow him and obey his commands, to go a step further. Loving as the world does is fine, but Jesus is calling his disciples to an even greater love.

Jesus' disciples are called to grow in faith and obedience. This uneasy love is part of that growth.

Jesus is calling us to this greater love, because he is love. His love is more demanding and it accomplishes greater things.

We know who the enemy is—whomever we find we are not in good will with. And we know why we are to love our enemies—because Jesus has commanded us to love them.

So, how can we love the enemy. *Love your enemies, do good to those who hate you, bless those who curse you, pray for those who abuse you?*

What is all that about? How can we do that? How can we wish well (bless) those that curse us? Or pray for those that abuse us?

Jesus has commanded it of us. That does not mean that we automatically have all the strength and wisdom to comply when we start following Jesus.

Jesus' command is setting the direction for his followers. He is telling them and us that "uneasy love" is the goal of our discipleship. It should give shape to our present, so that we will be able to come to the point in which all actions, thoughts, and imaginings are full of love.

This love won't happen easily and it won't happen on our own. It requires God's grace to work. It is a partnership between God and us.

We have to set our minds on being willing to act with love. Think about a ship on the sea. Each of us is the captain of a ship. The waters are pretty scary and dangerous. It takes much thought and effort to steer the ship rightly to keep it safe, but the ship can go nowhere without the wind filling its sails.

God's grace is the wind that fills the sails and moves the ship along. The ship needs both the captain and the wind to be able to get anywhere.

In like manner, it is a partnership between the believer and God that gives life and growth to this love.

On our own, we could not refocus our energies into good will for someone who has been abusive to us or someone whom we really dislike. But remember, this person is also a person for whom Jesus died!

Jesus values this person greatly and loves this person deeply and truly desires that we children love one another.

With Jesus' "uneasy love" we can refocus our hearts toward one another.

It is a shame when the actions of one person cause you or me to respond in kind. I really dislike it when I am somehow coerced into bad behavior. It happens, and afterwards I am really disgusted with myself for lowering myself to the level of the other.

If we are called to a more mature level of doing business as Christians, then when we get into the situation, we need to be on our guard to see how to love the other person. We love the other person because he/she needs our love.

They are missing something really special without our love. They need us. They need our love, our blessing, our prayers. "Uneasy love" is a goal. It is where we must to strive to be. It calls us to be a greater person than we naturally are. It calls us to love the unlovable. love.

I would like to share some examples of this.

I wonder if you have heard of Cory Ten Boom?

She was a maiden lady who lived with her sister, Betsy, and her father during the Second World War in Holland.

Cory's father was a clock and watchmaker, and the three of them lived in a very narrow, seven story house in Haarlem, Holland.

When Nazis began to come into their town, the Ten Booms provided a place for Jews to hide in a converted closet way up in their house. They were able to save the lives of dozens of Jews during that time, but one day the family was found out, and Cory, Betsy and their father were, themselves, taken to a work camp in Germany.

The camp was horrifying and degrading. Cory's father and sister died during the incarceration. Cory, along with all the women in the camp, were subjected to many humiliations. At various times they were forced to disrobe entirely and stand, freezing, in long lines while they were searched.

There were several guards who Cory remembered gaping at her and the other women as they stood in line freezing.

Cory survived the camp and was liberated at the end of the war. During her time there her faith in God had grown tremendously, especially her understanding of being thankful.

Cory was asked by church people in many places to come share her story. One day at such a meeting, Cory saw the face of one of the guards who had been in her camp, one who had caused her such humiliation and embarrassment.

The man had a nervous look in his eyes. Cory said that she walked up to the man, looked into his eyes and then reached out her hand and shook his. She told him that she forgave him for the pain he had caused her before and that she hoped that he had come to know that LORD Jesus.

The former guard knew he had received a gift of love that moment and he grew in his faith that day. Cory recognized this moment as a miracle, for she, in herself, could not have shaken the man's hand or forgiven him as she did.

But she knew God's love working in her made it possible. Cory's forgiveness helped both people grow in understanding of God's love that day. (She tells us that after the war the guard had come to faith; Cory's forgiving the man helped him to know that God had forgiven him, too.

Her forgiveness restored a broken relationship.

It sounds like Jesus is giving each disciple a command to grow in love, to act with uneasy love, but when a whole nation is confronted with overwhelming abuse, it, too is called to 'uneasy love".

I believe that such is the case of South Africa today:

That country was plagued by civil atrocities for so many years, while Apartheid was legal.

Apartheid was the law which separated white people and colored people and limited opportunity and citizen rights to coloreds. Somehow The South Africans had managed to get themselves into a terrible situation by declaring some people to be full citizens and others to have less than full citizenship or full freedom.

The white people who settled in SA from the mid 1600's came to be the citizens, and people of color (Asians, Arabs, brown and black colored natives) were distinguished and set apart from the whites.

Everyone had to carry papers with them to declare what level of rights they had. Colored people could work in the cities but they had to return to the villages, often to sub-human conditions every evening by nightfall.

To make matters worse, there was a police system that sought out and abused, tortured or killed any colored person who objected to the system.

This terrible abuse went on for decades.

Finally, the world placed a trade sanctions on South Africa, trying to force a change in their system.

It was not easy, it still has troubles, but in 1994 the Apartheid system was outlawed and a new governmental system established.

That year Nelson Mandela, who had been imprisoned for 27 years for leading the

African National Congress, became the first elected president of the new country.

The next year he appointed Archbishop Desmond Tutu to lead a Commission on Truth and Reconciliation. This commission is responsible for finding out the facts of the many abuses suffered during Apartheid."

Mr Dullah Omar, former Minister of Justice wrote:

> "a commission is a necessary exercise to enable South Africans to come to terms with their past on a morally accepted basis and to advance the cause of reconciliation."

> The commission decided that those who admitted to committing political crimes would be pardoned and those who remained silent could be prosecuted. Reparations to victims are being made by the new government.

> This Truth and Reconciliation Commission is striving to restore the community for their whole nation. They are trying to put into action this uneasy love that Jesus has commanded, so that their whole nation can be healed.

> Their task is enormous; I pray that the South Africans can accomplish what they have set out to do.

> The greatest example of "uneasy love" is the love that Jesus showed us when he died on the cross. He made the greatest sacrifice, his whole self, when he died for us. It was not an easy death. It was excruciating, humiliating,

and devastating, but he went to the cross for us to reestablish community between God and us. His death on the cross provided a way for humans to gather in community and grow in his love.

Jesus gave us the best example of loving the enemy that could be found. He calls us to do the same.

Luke 8: 26-39

²⁶ So they sailed over to the region of the Gerasenes, which is opposite Galilee. ²⁷ As Jesus stepped ashore, a certain man from the town met him who was possessed by demons. For a long time this man had worn no clothes and had not lived in a house, but among the tombs. ²⁸ When he saw Jesus, he cried out, fell down before him, and shouted with a loud voice, "Leave me alone, Jesus, Son of the Most High God! I beg you, do not torment me!" 29 For Jesus had started commanding the evil spirit to come out of the man. (For it had seized him many times, so he would be bound with chains and shackles and kept under guard. But he would break the restraints and be driven by the demon into deserted places.) 30 Jesus then asked him, "What is your name?" He said, "Legion," because many demons had entered him. 31 And they began to beg him not to order them to depart into the abyss. 32 Now a large herd of pigs was feeding there on the hillside, and the demonic spirits begged Jesus to let them go into them. He gave them permission. 33 So the demons came out

of the man and went into the pigs, and the herd of pigs rushed down the steep slope into the lake and drowned. 34 When the herdsmen saw what had happened, they ran off and spread the news in the town and countryside. 35 So the people went out to see what had happened, and they came to Jesus. They found the man from whom the demons had gone out, sitting at Jesus' feet, clothed and in his right mind, and they were afraid. 36 Those who had seen it told them how the man who had been demon-possessed had been healed. 37 Then all the people of the Gerasenes and the surrounding region asked Jesus to leave them alone, for they were seized with great fear. So he got into the boat and left. 38 The man from whom the demons had gone out begged to go with him, but Jesus sent him away, saying, 39 "Return to your home, and declare what God has done for you." So he went away, proclaiming throughout the whole town what Jesus had done for him.

BUT FOR THE GRACE OF GOD ...

Mother used to be an English and social studies teacher in junior high. She told me about one of her students, who was about to graduate from eighth grade. He came into her room one afternoon and said something like: "I've been looking at this world map for a year now and there's something that really puzzles me. I wonder ... when you sail in a boat across the Indian Ocean to China and further, here, to the edge of the map, what happens then?"

We can laugh at the student's misunderstanding, but I think we also know that we don't know everything ourselves!

Some of us are now into computers. If you've spent much time with computers, you know that there is some part of a computer's functioning that falls under the category of the 'unknown'. We may finally decide that there are some things about a computer we just don't understand!

The story we're looking at today, deals, in part, with another unknown--demons. We don't use the word demon today as people did in Bible times. Back then people used the word demon to describe the cause of the troubles that plagued them. (Maybe it's kind of like how we use the word 'germ' for what causes the flu or cold. But it was used even more broadly.) Demon was a useful word to explain what caused everything from headaches, to convulsions, to mental illness, to loss of sight or hearing; demons were even blamed for natural calamities.

This story is about a man who was filled with demons, 6,000 demons. The story of the Gerasene Demoniac is a story of a very wretched person. I admit that the idea of someone who has no control over his mind, his body, or his tongue is very distressing to me! Such a person, in such an awful state, might prompt me to say, "There, but for the Grace of God, go I."

I can imagine that the people of the city of Gerasa had many of the same feelings that I did when I heard about the man. They didn't know what to do with him! He was out of control! He was stronger than any chains they could put on him. He ran around stark, buck naked! He tore off any clothes that people tried to put on him. The many voices within him drove him all over the countryside, screaming at whatever was in his way! The terrified people may have wondered if he might not hurt them or their children, even as he continued to hurt himself. The man lived in the graveyard among the tombs, among the dead. (The people were probably relieved that he wasn't constantly in their sight, reminding them of his problems.)

At the same time, while this was going on in Gerasa, on the far side of the Sea of Galilee, Jesus and his disciples had taken a boat onto the sea. Their trip across the sea to gentile territory had been one they would never forget. You see, there had been a wild storm that came up quite suddenly and nearly sank their boat. But Jesus had rebuked the wind and the sea, and everything became still! The danger was gone! The disciples were amazed and afraid. They wondered among themselves what sort of man could have control over even such great forces as the wind and sea. That sort of authority could only come from God!

When their boat landed, they were in Gerasene territory. The man possessed of demons was there. When Jesus saw the man, he commanded the demons to leave him. The demons answered by saying, *"What have you to do with me, Jesus, Son of the Most High God? I beg you, do not torment me".* The demons within the man already knew who Jesus was and that he had authority over them. Jesus asked the name of the man. He replied, "Legion, for there are many of us." (He used the word legion because a legion was a Roman military unit of 6,000 fighting men.) You can see that this man was seriously afflicted by many inner, fighting voices.

Legion then pleaded with Jesus to allow them to go into a large herd of pigs which was nearby. Jesus allowed this, and suddenly the pigs raced over a cliff into the lake, drowning!

I can imagine what the conversation was like among the pig herders. "Did you see that! What happened? I can't believe it! What in the world got into the animals? Did you see anything that could have spooked them? What'll we do now? We sure can't get them back--they're gone! Who's gonna pay for this?

The whole town is gonna be mad!" The herders went running all over the countryside, telling anyone that would listen about how their pigs had run over the cliff and drowned. This brought the people out to see what had happened.

When the townspeople got to the scene, they might not have noticed the man right away. After all, they were used to seeing the man running around in his altogethers, creating commotion. As the Gerasene man sat at Jesus' feet, he didn't stick out. They may have done a 'double take'. "Was this the crazy man? It couldn't be! This man was dressed". (Somehow seeing someone out of context makes it difficult to recognize the person.) The Gerasene man was out of context, and they probably had to look again to be sure he was the same person.

That wretched man, who had plagued them for so long, had changed! He was calmly seated at the feet of some Jew, maybe a teacher; he was dressed, and he was apparently in his right mind!

When the people did recognize the man, and were told how he had been changed, they became afraid! They realized that this man, this menace to their community, was now different. Something had happened to the man to give him back his sanity.

That was something that they couldn't do. (They hadn't even been able to keep him restrained!) Some very powerful force, a force much stronger than any of them, was at work here! Then they began to realize that the loss of the pig herd was somehow related to the change in the crazy man. This made them really afraid! They asked Jesus to leave.

The man, on the other hand, was discovering new life through healing. He was now in his right mind.

He no longer heard thousands of angry voices in his mind ordering him to run, hurt, fear or fight. He could now begin to see the world with his sanity restored. The man had begun a whole new life, through his new relationship with Jesus. He recognized Jesus as the one who gave him this new life. Jesus had healed him completely! He had been touched by Jesus' grace.

The people of Gerasa were frightened by the power they saw. They sent Jesus away and didn't receive a blessing from him. They were stuck in their terror.

Whereas the demoniac had been healed by the grace of God and came to know Jesus, the townspeople only feared him. They didn't want him anywhere near them! They are the ones who missed the Grace of God, because they didn't reach out for it. They are the ones about whom we could say, "They missed the Grace of God."

Before Jesus left, the man, who was now healed of demon possession, begged to go with him. But Jesus told him, "Return home, and declare how much God has done for you."

I think I can appreciate how the Gerasene man felt then. His life had been a pure, hellish nightmare before Jesus came. Suddenly, his sanity had returned! He wanted to remain with Jesus, to go wherever Jesus went, to take up his new life in Jesus' company.

But Jesus had another plan for him. He sent the man back to his city with a message to proclaim how much God had done for him.

I wonder if the man struggled at this point--to

turn back to Gerasa, leaving Jesus to return to Palestine. I think we can empathize with the man. Aren't our own lives like that? We, too, must live our lives as believers in Christ, but we can't join Jesus in Palestine. We can't sit at Jesus' feet and enjoy his company. We, too, have been given a commission to go into our world and proclaim the Good News--to tell what God has done for US.

Scripture tells us that the man went away, proclaiming throughout the city how much Jesus had done for him. It seems that the Gerasene man knew that what God had done for him is what Jesus had done for him. Jesus has God's power. Jesus had authority to calm the storm at sea. Jesus had the authority to command the demons to leave the man, and Jesus had the authority to make the man whole. The power and authority that God has is the same power and authority that Jesus has!

There were two responses to Jesus in this story. There was the Gerasene man, whose life was wonderfully changed. He returned to his city proclaiming what Jesus had done for him. And there were the townspeople who were afraid and asked Jesus to leave them alone.

Which are we like? Are we, like the townsfolk, fearful of what an encounter with Jesus would mean to us? Do we push Jesus away? Do we say, "No, not now, not yet. I'd rather deal with the demons I know, than to meet you, Jesus. Are we afraid to ask Jesus into our lives--to be a healing and loving presence within us?

Or, are we like the man of Gerasa, experiencing the

healing power of Christ? Do we have a story to proclaim about what Christ has done for us? Do we share the power of Christ with others?

I know several of our members here who have come through serious illnesses this past year and are with us today to tell us of God's good work in their lives. There are others of us who have experienced the healing touch of the Lord in their lives.

I titled this sermon, "but for the Grace of God...". I think, now, I'd like to say because of the Grace of God. We have been healed, physically and spiritually, and have a commission to go into our world, declaring what God has done for us!

Luke 10:25-37

25 On one occasion an expert in the law stood up to test Jesus. "Teacher," he asked, "what must I do to inherit eternal life?"

26 "What is written in the Law?" he replied. "How do you read it?"

27 He answered, "Love the Lord your God with all your heart and with all your soul and with all your strength and with all your mind[a]; and, 'Love your neighbor as yourself.[b]"

28 "You have answered correctly," Jesus replied. "Do this and you will live."

29 But he wanted to justify himself, so he asked Jesus, "And who is my neighbor?"

30 In reply Jesus said: "A man was going down from Jerusalem to Jericho, when he was attacked by robbers. They stripped him of his clothes, beat him and went away, leaving him half dead. 31 A priest happened to be going down

the same road, and when he saw the man, he passed by on the other side. *32* So too, a Levite, when he came to the place and saw him, passed by on the other side.

33 But a Samaritan, as he traveled, came where the man was; and when he saw him, he took pity on him. *34* He went to him and bandaged his wounds, pouring on oil and wine. Then he put the man on his own donkey, brought him to an inn and took care of him. *35* The next day he took out two denarii[c] and gave them to the innkeeper. 'Look after him,' he said, 'and when I return, I will reimburse you for any extra expense you may have.'

36 "Which of these three do you think was a neighbor to the man who fell into the hands of robbers?"

37 The expert in the law replied, "The one who had mercy on him."

Jesus told him, "Go and do likewise."

DOING LIKEWISE

The lawyer found Jesus surrounded by a crowd.
That was to be expected. He managed to work
his way through the crowd and finally he was
within earshot of Jesus, so he called out to him.
*"Teacher, tell me, what must I do to inherit
eternal life?"*

The crowd opened up a bit to allow the lawyer to
come closer to the teacher. Jesus gazed into the
lawyer's eyes and asked him, *"Tell us what the
law says."*

This was not a trick question from Jesus. That was
the way conversation went among the Jews. They
would question to one another--one question
would be answered with another.

The lawyer answered exactly right, quoting the
Shema, the great Law: *"You must love the Lord,
your God, with all your heart, soul, mind, and
strength."*

And, in a flash of insight, the lawyers added, *"and
love your neighbor as yourself."*

Jesus nodded and smiled at the lawyer. *"You
have answered rightly. Go and do."*

But the lawyer returned yet another question.

Being a lawyer, wanting to know exactly what the
law required, he asked, *"And who is my neighbor?"*

Jesus saw within the lawyer the mind of a well-
studied man, one who was exacting with the words
of the law. The lawyer was looking for a precise

definition of "neighbor," the one whom he was to love like his own body. The lawyer also already believed he knew who his neighbor was:

His neighbor was a son of Abraham. More specifically, the neighbor was a fellow Jew, a member of the ruling class--a lawyer, a scribe, a Pharisee, a priest, a Levite, maybe a rabbi. Of course, the lawyer's own family would be considered his neighbor, how much closer could someone get?

These folks the lawyer believed to be his neighbors. He could understand the law that told him to love these as he loved himself.

It is interesting to note that the greatest commandment, and its corollary, were given in Matthew and Mark from Jesus. There was no following parable as is found in Luke. But Jesus does add, *"on this hang all the law and the prophets."*

Then Jesus answered the lawyer's second question with a story:

There was a certain man who traveled down to Jericho, from Jerusalem, a winding and dangerous journey over perilous road. The road was especially notorious for the brigands that often attacked travelers in that wilderness.

On this day, as the man made his way over the rough stones along the dusty path, he was suddenly overpowered by several strong men. The men beat him and kicked him terribly; they pulled his robes and undergarments off him, leaving him naked, stole his pack, everything he had taken for his journey, and left him for dead on the side of the road.

After some time passed more steps were heard coming down the road. The long robes of a priest swished and swept along the dirt path. As the priest approached, he saw the bloodied body of the man. He was not sure what to do for this man, if indeed anything could be done. The man was probably dead or would be soon. The priest carefully passed by the wounded man, perhaps saying something like, "I hope someone will be better able to help the man."

The sun beat down hot on the road. Desert heat is nothing to be out in, but after more time passed, another stranger came upon the scene. This traveler was a Levite, a man who worked in the Temple. The Levite saw the near-dead man, too, but he passed by him on the other side.

The lawyer listened carefully to the story. He could understand how it was with these different travelers. He could guess that the priest would have the Law first on his mind, if he even touched them man, he would then be "unclean" and would not be able to perform his duties as a priest. And the Levite might have thought that the bloodied man's body was really a trap, planted there by thieves, to catch single, unwary travelers.

The lawyer could certainly understand their dilemma. The man on the road really wasn't their concern. They had to watch out for their own business first. Maybe someone else would come by and care for the man.

I have failed the compassion test at different times. One time as I was walking up to the grocery store, I noticed a man in a wheel chair near the entry door.

There were two elementary-aged children apparently with him. As I got closer to the entry, I noticed that the man held a large tin can for collections and there was a sign near him, saying "for a new wheel chair". The wheel chair he sat in was a very old sort. Not with the modern electric advantages. When I was up close to the man, I could see that he had no legs, almost no lower body. He was very thin and bent and obviously had some serious problems. Before I actually got close to the man, the children had moved away from him. I began to think "Yes, this man certainly needs a good, modern wheel chair, but isn't there some organization that provides them to needy people, for free? Then I found myself thinking, I wonder if this is a scam. The man certainly needs help, but I don't know if the wheel chair he's sitting in is the only one he has. I rather think he's using the oldest one around to gain sympathy. The man already had my sympathy, but I wondered about the scam. The man never caught my eye. I think I would have given him something, but he didn't seem interested in me as a potential donor. I don't know. I think I failed the compassion test that morning. I shouldn't judge a person in need, but there I certainly did.

We have many opportunities to take the compassion test these days. I think I'm not alone in failing the test. That's one of the problems today. The point of the Good Samaritan story was that the first two respectable people who might have helped the dying man, found reasons to walk by on the other side.

We all have our reasons to pass by on the

other side, too. We may think that we simply do not have time to help. (Time is a major theme with us these days. We beg off of many things because of time.) We may fear that we could get hurt by stopping--maybe the person in need could hurt us, or maybe the neighborhood is dangerous and another dangerous person might appear

We may fear what others might say about our stopping in that neighborhood, or being with that sort of person. We might think that if we get involved, it will cost us too much, more than we think we can give. What if we catch some dreaded disease? That's a reason.

What if one of our friends tells us off and walks away because of our actions? What if word gets around that we are associating with the wrong sort?

The lawyer wanted to be able to have some say in whom he would help. He wanted to discount those who were not like him.

The story continued:

Another man appeared on the road; he didn't look like either the Priest or the Levite. His dress was different, his head covering was different; if we were familiar with the clothes of the day we would have recognized the man as a Samaritan, a man of mixed- race, Israelite and Assyrian. The Samaritans were enemies of the Jews. They were the result of the Assyrian invasion hundreds of years before, when the Assyrians plundered and exiled many of the tribes of Israel and then intermarried with the remaining Israelites, making them no longer purely children of Abraham. They even worshiped differently than did the Jews. They were considered second-class people, not worthy of anything.

The Samaritan man was far from home. He had taken his animal and his pack and traveled toward Jericho, which put him on this difficult road. As he was walking he saw the figure a ways from him lying in the dust. The closer he got, the more he could see; it was a man, bleeding and badly wounded.

The Samaritan man stopped and listened, maybe wondering if there were others in the area. He didn't hear anything. It seems the two were alone.

The Samaritan carefully approached the man and looked at him. Then he squatted down and touched the man, rolling him over gently. He could just barely see the man was breathing. The Samaritan man felt great compassion for this poor creature that was oozing life before him. He could almost feel the pain of the bruises and cuts on his own body.

The Samaritan got up and went to the pack on his beast and took out wine and oil. He poured the wine over the open cuts, cleansing them with the alcohol; then he poured oil over the man's bruises.

Then the Samaritan man struggled and picked up the man and set him on his beast. Eventually, the Samaritan found an inn where the man could rest and heal. He gave the innkeeper two coins, worth two day's wages, to care for the man, and promised to pay further costs when he returned.

Jesus looked at the lawyer, who had been

listening carefully to Jesus' story. Jesus asked, *"Who would you say was the neighbor?"*

The lawyer answered, *"The man who showed mercy."*

Jesus smiled and said, *"Go and do likewise."* The neighbor was the man who showed mercy, who had compassion for the wounded man.

The neighbor was the man who had responded to the need of the man on the road. The neighbor was the man who was tuned to God's leading, to do God's will in the world. The neighbor could not be recognized by his race, or his clothing, or his standing in the community. The neighbor was the one who had compassion, who showed mercy.

Jesus tore down the old definition of neighbor. His focus was not the man in the road who needed help, although, the man did need help. As Christians we are called to lend a hand and give help to whoever is in need.

But the point of Jesus' message to the lawyer was that the neighbor was the man who had compassion, who was merciful.

That man, who was a Samaritan, was a person after God's own heart.

That man, the Samaritan, looked with compassion on the wounded man, just as God was looking at the man.

That man, the Samaritan, was in tune with God's desire that the wounded man be helped.

That man, the Samaritan, not only saw the problem

and was aware of it. The Samaritan, did something about the problem. He acted on the man's behalf and took good care of him. That Samaritan man was the neighbor.

The lawyer had asked what the requirement was for inheriting eternal life, and his answer was correct. Jesus told him so. The answer was to love God with all your heart, your mind, your soul, and your strength, and to love your neighbor as yourself.

The good news in this Scripture is that Jesus showed us our neighbor, that is the ones who are listening to God's voice. The good news is that old barriers between people have been broken down.

Neighbors come in many packagings nowadays. Jesus tells us that the one who showed mercy on the beaten man was the neighbor.

The man happened to be a Samaritan; a man who was considered unclean, unworthy, in fact despised and hated. But the Samaritan man was the one who heard the voice of God calling to reach out and help the man in need. He was the only one on the road that day who answered God's call to be in ministry. He was the one who was familiar with God's voice and disciplined enough to know what he needed to do.

The Samaritan man did not spend time and energy worrying about how much time it would take to help. He did not worry about the money he would need to shell out at the inn or how much more it would cost him to make up for any further expenses. He did not worry that the man was not from his world, that the man might even be his enemy. The Samaritan man just did what needed to be done. He was doing the will of God.

Such a person is our neighbor. Jesus said that we are to love our neighbors as we love our own selves. Our neighbors are those who show mercy, those who are listening to God and following God's direction.

Remember the time when Jesus was with his disciples in someone's house, and his family, his mother and brothers and sisters came to the house and asked to speak to Jesus. Jesus was told of his family wanting him outside, and his reply was a question, which he answered himself.

> ""Who is my mother, and who are my brothers?" And pointing to his disciples, he said, "Here are my mother and my brothers! For whoever does the will of my Father in heaven is my brother and sister and mother."

Jesus' final words to the lawyer give us marching orders, too. He said, "go and do likewise." We are told to be like the Good Neighbor, the Samaritan man, and listen for God's voice, see the need and address it, whenever we can.

Second ending to Good Samaritan
parable:

(GOLDEN BRICKS)

I can imagine the crowd, the lawyer too, were
shaking their heads at this last piece to the story.
They could have gone in for an ordinary person
being the hero in the story, but a Samaritan man!
That was unexpected, and the thought of him doing
kindness to the injured man may have even made
them sick inside.

There was enmity between the two cultures back
then, the same as it is today between the Jews in
Israel and the Palestinians. It was a shock to hear
Jesus use such a man in the story.

We started this with a question. I said the whole
thing began with a question that the lawyer asked
Jesus. That is true, but the first question that the
lawyer asked Jesus wasn't about his neighbor,
but about inheriting eternal life. The lawyer
asked, "What must I do to inherit eternal life?"

Then Jesus answered the lawyer with another
question, just the way the Jews did back then.
[They loved to talk in questions, one question
answering another question.]

Jesus asked, "What do you find in Scripture?"

And the lawyer immediately responded with
two well-known verses from the Torah—
one in Deuteronomy and one in Leviticus:

You shall love the Lord your God with all your
heart, with all your soul, with all your strength
and with all your mind. And "You shall love
your neighbor as yourself."

The interesting thing here, though, is that this same picture is mentioned in Matthew's Gospel in a slightly different way.

In Matthew Jesus is asked by some Pharisees who were trying to trip him up in some tricky questions, "What is the greatest commandment?"

And Jesus answered that question with the same two commandments that the lawyer in Luke says. You shall love your God with all your heart, with all your soul and with all your might. [Actually, Jesus even added mind to the other strengths we are to love God with.]

And Jesus went right on saying, *"and the second [greatest command] is like it, You shall love your neighbor as yourself."*

And Jesus continued, *"on these two hang all the law and the prophets."* That's quite a mouthful! All the law and the prophets, that would mean that everything in sacred writing is wrapped up in those two ideas—to love God and to love others as ourselves.

But in Matthew there is even another scripture in chapter 7, when Jesus gives the command to do unto others as you would have others do unto you. And Jesus added then, that that command sums all the law and the prophets.

Do you suppose Jesus was confused? Why is he saying this is all the law and the prophets and that is all the law and the prophets, and why is Luke using the same verses with the lawyer answering Jesus and in Matthew Jesus answering the Pharisees.

I don't think we have a problem here at all, but I do think we've found the core of Jesus' message to us. I think that Jesus probably spoke many times about this command to love God and neighbor as ourselves. It was probably told many times in different settings, and Matthew remembered two times when Jesus spoke it and Luke had a different memory of Jesus working with that message.

Love God with all your heart, all your soul, all your strength and all your mind. That pretty much sums up all the different ways we can do anything. Jesus was quoting the Shema, the favorite verse in Deut. 6:4-5. It was so important to the Jews that they made tiny little scrolls with the verse on it and put them in phylacteries, little leather boxes and tied them on their foreheads and left arms before they went to prayer.

The Shema was also in little scrolls on the doorposts of every house. Everyone who entered the house would touch the little box and remember the words: *You shall love the Lord your God with all your heart, with all your soul and with all your might.*"

The Greatest Commandment is to love God … in every way we can with all the resources we have been given. That's what God requires of us.

That's a tall command. It was not a big surprise that Jesus knew the answer to that question.

It was not even surprising that Jesus coupled that verse with the one in Lev. 19:18—*you shall love your neighbor as yourself.*

Actually, when we look at the two verses: love

your neighbor as yourself and do unto others as you would have them do to you, it's the same command, stated slightly differently. Both others/neighbor and self are included. We are to treat others as we would like to be treated or how we do treat ourselves.

Jesus was saying that the two are the same and that they are a corollary to the first command to love God with all we have.

What is important for us today to know is that in Luke we have a dynamic picture of this love.

In the parable of the Good Samaritan we see love in action. We discover that love is far from an emotion; love is an action verb; love is all about building up the other person. That's what love is.

The Samaritan man took from his own limited provisions to clean and bind up the wounds of the man. He took the man to an inn where the man could get more help as he recovered, and he saw to it that the man's needs would be met even in his absence by giving the 2 denarius to the inn keeper. The Samaritan man was doing everything he could to build back the man who had been hurt.

That's what love means—not some sentimental, dripping emotion, but the swift thoughtful action toward someone who is in need. Love is all about building up the other.

Think about it. When we live in a family and in a community of others, how much of the time do we spend helping build up others?

There are hundreds of good ways to build up others. (Notice that I'm changing the word "love" for "build up". Sometimes it can help us to see more clearly by using a different term that doesn't have the same baggage on it. So let's think of "love" as "Building Up" of others.

We build up others by a smile on our faces when we see them. It gives them a positive feeling that they are a pleasure to see and encourages them.

We build up others by a kind word. We build up others by encouraging them in their efforts. I strongly believe family members need to encourage and give room to one another to grow in their unique gifts and talents.

We build up others by helping them see the error of their ways.(That's a parental love, which is sometimes required.

Sometimes we find someone who is laying on our path, and we have the choice of walking by on the other side, of ignoring the need. That is not the way to build up someone, and we may very well be judged someday for doing that.

The possibilities are endless … of finding a need to help build up another. Let us be on the lookout for them.

Luke 10:38-42

[38] Now as they went on their way, Jesus entered a certain village where a woman named Martha welcomed him as a guest. [39] She had a sister named Mary, who sat at the Lord's feet and listened to what he said. [40] But Martha was distracted with all the preparations she had to make, so she came up to him and said, "Lord, don't you care that my sister has left me to do all the work alone? Tell her to help me." [41] But the Lord answered her, "Martha, Martha, you are worried and troubled about many things, [42] but one thing is needed. Mary has chosen the best part; it will not be taken away from her."

AT HIS FEET

Martha was busy. She was the sort of woman who could do many things, and whatever she did she did well. She was a wonderful homemaker, a wonderful cook, and a wonderful hostess. She may have been a wonderful seamstress and a great gardener as well. As the big sister, Martha had been responsible for their household for a number of years. She was widely known for her gracious hospitality and lovely home. Anyone who had an opportunity to sample Martha's cooking or her welcoming way would remember it with pleasure.

Today was special. Martha and her siblings, Lazarus and Mary, were expecting a very special guest. They had known about Jesus' visit for some time, but they didn't know for sure which day he would arrive. They had become acquainted with Jesus a while back, but now he was coming to be with them in their home.

Having Jesus visit them was more than exciting. Of course, when Jesus came he would not come alone. No, he had disciples who went everywhere with him. The followers could easily curl up in a corner somewhere to sleep, but meals would be a major consideration while they were visiting.

Martha had cooked for big groups before, but this group might require several meals during their stay.

Martha had made careful plans for their visit.

She and her sister had already gone to the
market and purchased necessary items
that they couldn't get from their own
garden. Much had been prepared in
advance of the company's arrival.

Finally, the guests were here. They had arrived late
in the afternoon, but they were in time for dinner. Of
course, besides Jesus, their good friend and
special guest of honor, and his followers, there
were a number of towns' people who showed up at
the house to hear the young rabbi. They had heard
about his teaching and healing before, and now he
had come to their own town of Bethany. These
towns' folk jammed into the house and began
gathering around Jesus.

When Jesus sat down to teach; the crowd
scooched in closer to hear him. Martha looked
around for her sister Mary; she wanted her to help
in the final details of the dinner. But where was
she?

Martha looked in several places and finally saw
Mary, sitting at Jesus' feet, listening intently to his
words.

"How could she do that?" thought Martha. How can
she leave me high and dry without her help with all
these people I'm responsible for?

Martha couldn't believe that Mary would leave her
in this very busy moment, so she decided to go to
Jesus and ask his help. Surely, he would
understand the problem and quickly set Mary

straight. (It would serve Mary right if she were a little embarrassed about it.)

Martha edged around the room and finally was able to stand next to Jesus' chair. She said, "Lord, do you not care that my sister has left me to do all the work by myself? Tell her then to help me."

But Jesus turned to Martha and spoke to her.

He said, *"Martha, Martha, you are worried and distracted by many things; there is need of only one thing. Mary has chosen the better part, which will not be taken away from her."*

I'd like us to think back a moment to last week.

We looked at the scripture verse that comes just before Mary and Martha--Luke's parable of the Good Samaritan. We discovered that before Jesus told that parable he had been talking with a lawyer who was interested in discovering how one can inherit eternal life.

Jesus had asked the lawyer to tell him what the Bible said about it, and the lawyer said, *"You shall love the Lord with all your heart, with all your soul, with all your strength and with all your mind; and you shall love your neighbor as yourself. "*

Jesus told the lawyer that was right, *"Do this and you shall live—[inherit eternal life.]"*

Love God in every way you can, and your neighbor as yourself.

Love God and neighbor.

(These same two verses were spoken by Jesus

in two different places in Matthew. He identified them as the sum of all the law and the prophets.)

Then Jesus told the parable of the Samaritan man who cared so well for the Jew, spending his resources and time on him. That was Jesus' picture of a good neighbor, one who was responsible to love those in need.

Last week I talked about love as an act of building up the other person. Doing whatever you can to build the other person up. Good Sam was about building up the wounded traveler—a stranger, even an enemy who was in need.

The very next scene is Jesus coming to the home in Bethany, where Mary and Martha and Lazarus lived. I don't think that Luke accidentally placed that story next. We might even think of them as bookend pictures—one of loving our neighbor and the other of loving God.

Mary came to Jesus' feet and sat down to hear him. I can just see her slipping herself, casually, right there down in front of Jesus and took a seat on the floor. (Jesus was probably in a chair, as teachers taught from the position of sitting on a chair.)

Mary had come to Jesus' feet, to sit and learn from him to soak up his wisdom, goodness, and love. She was taking the opportunity to be with Jesus right then, even though there were pressing things to do elsewhere. She was taking the time for herself to be built up by him. It was not a selfish thing to do; it was the right thing to do. That's what Jesus told Martha.

We can't be loving—hear 'building others up'—when we are running low of love ourselves. We have to connect to the source of love, sit at Jesus' feet, and drink in his love, his wisdom, his forgiveness, his guidance … his vision for our future before we can possibly by effective as builders of others.

If we define love as building up of others, helping them to be more in every way. That's possible to do for others, but how might we build up God? That doesn't work. God is already God. There is no building up … or is there? God made us, in God's image we were created. And we were created for God, to be God's friends. So maybe the loving/building up is about letting God build us up.

Letting God do his work in us, to make us more what God wants us to be.

When we come to Jesus' feet—that is when we subject ourselves to him, coming humbly before him to receive what he has for us, we are in the position of receiving blessings. We receive forgiveness and a new life. We receive guidance and encouragement. Jesus begins to build us into the people he wants us to be.

Martha had been busy working to serve the many neighbors who had come to her house. She was totally caught up in service, yet she was missing the key thing, the most important thing. She had been doing something good, instead of being with the best.

You know, Martha was an upright woman who was doing everything she could to be a proper hostess in her own home and to make her guests welcome and comfortable during their stay.

Sometimes when I hear a list of sins I don't see that I fall into those categories. For instance, Paul tells the Galatians 5:*19Now the works of the flesh are obvious: fornication, impurity, licentiousness, 20idolatry, sorcery, enmities, strife, jealousy, anger, quarrels, dissensions, factions, 21envy,☐ drunkenness, carousing, and things like these. (I am warning you, as I warned you before: those who do such things will not inherit the kingdom of God.)*

Martha was not being bad. She was not being wicked, or ugly; or sinful, or dangerous. She was not a liar, a cheat, a sexual deviant, a thief, a drug dealer, a pornographer. She wasn't running a brothel or some underground baby-selling racket.

What was Martha's problem? Martha was so wrapped up in the stuff of doing her job, that she missed Jesus. She was missing a golden moment. She was missing being in Jesus' presence and getting to know him. When she was serving him, she wasn't necessarily growing closer to him. Jesus was in her home, in her midst, and she was washing dishes and looking for her sister to help get out the dessert.

We can learn much from this lesson in Luke, from both the Good Samaritan and Mary and Martha. They are both pictures of love—loving neighbor and loving God in Christ.

I redefined 'love' for us last week as building up of others, doing everything you can to build up and not to tear down. That's what love is about. We are loving one another when we build one another up, regardless of any differences.

We love God by allowing God to build us up in faith. That requires our being there at his feet—listening to him, learning from him, receiving forgiveness from him and worshiping him only.

It's amazing how far society has come from those simple Bible times, before electricity and industrialization and modern inventions, and all. But we are not all that different from Martha.

Most of us allow ourselves to be influenced by activities that take us from the feet of Jesus. We have a zillion reasons why we miss opportunities to study Jesus in Bible and worship him in Christian fellowship. Those reasons might be good reasons, but they are missing the BEST there is, and that is taking the second commandment before the first.

That might not play well … down the road.

Spending time at the feet of Jesus—studying his word in the Bible, growing together in faith and fellowship, are not nice to haves, they are necessary to the growth of a Christian. We have to find those times, when like Mary, we can be there at the Lord's feet, learning, growing, worshiping him. Perhaps I'm preaching to the choir today, but we all need to hear this message. In fact, I believe this message should be our new year's vision for our church.

Luke 12: 13-21

[13] One of the multitude said to him, "Teacher, bid my brother divide the inheritance with me."[14] But he said to him, "Man, who made me a judge or divider over you?"[15] And he said to them, "Take heed, and beware of all covetousness; for a man's life does not consist in the abundance of his possessions."

<u>BEING RICH TOWARD GOD</u>

Right now, at this very moment at Rayne
Memorial UMC in New Orleans the church is
celebrating the re-opening of their sanctuary.
It has been closed since Katrina hit almost
two years ago. The great steeple above their
sanctuary blew down, causing much damage.
They have been repairing it all this time. This
morning is their jubilant re-opening of their
beautiful worship space.

It's been nearly two years since Hurricane
Katrina left such great devastation on the gulf
coast. We've heard much about it; some of us
have lived closely to it; many of us have tried
to help out in some way for those who lost so
much. We gave money to help the relief
effort. There is yet much work to be done.

I am very sure that for the people who lived on
the gulf coast and went through Katrina that
event will be the 'LIFE-SHAPING' event of their
lives. Already the people refer to their "Pre-K"
and "Post-K" worlds. There are great differences
in those two worlds.

I remember knowing a Baptist pastor and his
family who had been living in Tehran doing
mission work in the '70's when they were
forced to leave everything they owned and
race to the airport to escape the new regime
that had taken over the country. They simply
locked their apartment door, hoping that they
MIGHT someday be able to return and

collect their stuff. I used to think that family had suffered terribly. What a horrible thing to lose everything you owned—overnight. I was very impressed that a family could lose so much.

Come to think of it, I must have been very naïve to think this only happened to one family, one time—ever! History is full of such trouble that has happened to entire communities.

Then Katrina happened. The devastation is more than we can understand, because of the enormity of the loss. I didn't try to get numbers of how many houses were affected by the storm and then the flood, but it was a very large number. People lost everything they owned. Nothing was left. Some even lost their friends and family members.

The magnitude of the loss is so great it is impossible to conceive. The flood was almost two years ago, but there are many people who seem to be stuck in the memory of their loss. They can't seem to move on to a new life, because they are still struggling with their personal loss. They know they were devastated, and they are stuck in that devastation. [Now hold that thought.]

Jesus was talking to the crowd one day when a man nudged his way forward and asked Jesus to help him. The man was apparently engaged in a dispute about his father's estate. He was probably the younger son, and he felt he was not getting a fair share of his dad's estate.

I believe that same story has been repeated many, many times over generations. I remember that happened in my mother's family. Mother's grandmother and her brother had stayed on the farm in Eastern Canada, taking care of their parents and working the farm. But after the parents passed and the will was read, the entire estate went to an older brother who had left home when he was still a teen. He was the first child, and the rule of primogeniture prevailed. The two who had stayed at home, worked the farm, and cared for their parents got nothing.

I'm sure there are many stories like that could be heard even right here among us.

Jesus looked at the man who had asked him for justice, but rather than acting as a judge over that case, Jesus used the subject of ownership as an opportunity to spend some time on an important subject.

Jesus told a story about a farmer, a well-to-do farmer:

Seems the farmer had done well in the past, but when the new harvest was complete, he had quite a surprise. The harvest was far greater than he expected, even in his wildest dreams he wouldn't have expected such a great harvest.

So suddenly there was a problem. What should he do with all the crops that he now had? What could he do to care for all this newfound wealth?

The farmer already had barns filled to overflowing with the crops, and it was not nearly enough. He needed more. "Well", thought the farmer, "I know what I'll do. I'll just tear down these old barns and build much bigger ones. And then I'll have room to store all my crops and I'll be able to kick back and enjoy the fruits of all my labors."

Then the farmer got to dreaming. He could just see himself lying in a chaise lounge, a glass of sweet tea in his hand and BBQ on the grill. He would have the easy life now. It was all his for the enjoying. It was as if he had won the lottery, big time. He had no more worries now. He was about to have it all—the good life, everything he had ever wanted, right at his fingertips.

He could travel all he wanted. He could get that new Beemer with the souped-up motor. He could get all new clothes. Nothing was too much for him.

Nothing would be too expensive now. He had struck it rich.

And he was pleased with himself. How lucky he was--how incredibly lucky!

All this was in the farmer's mind as he dozed off to sleep that night. Yes, he was a lucky man, indeed.

What a great difference between those two situations!

At first glance the two seem completely opposite from one another. You have the people who lost everything in Katrina's ravaging, and then there's the farmer who struck it rich overnight. Those are two completely opposite problems, right?

But! I think that both the rich man and some of the victims of Katrina have something in common. Both of them were looking at STUFF the wrong way. They held too much value on STUFF.

It's a hard lesson to learn.

Surely there's not one of us here who doesn't value the gifts that God has given us, and doesn't that include our stuff?

How can your pastor stand here and say we shouldn't value our stuff? What is it that we work so hard to get, if it isn't our stuff?

Do you see a problem with that? Is obtaining and keeping STUFF the whole reason we exist? Is that what gives happiness? Is STUFF what is important in life?

There's a problem with that sort of thinking.

The problem is when we think too much of STUFF we are falling into the same unhealthy place that the rich man and some of the Katrina sufferers have fallen.

We are then greedy people.

That's what the rich farmer discovered ... too late. He had accumulated so much, and he couldn't see anything except his STUFF. He looked at the STUFF and thought how happy it would make him. He thought how easily he now could live. 'Eat, drink and be merry ... for the rest of my life'. That's what he thought. He was now on Easy Street. He had no worries. He had no reason to struggle or work. He had it all!

Although the survivors of Katrina felt just the opposite, because they had just lost everything, those who were completely devastated by their loss found they couldn't move beyond it. They had set such value on their STUFF and they were so sorry for themselves for losing their STUFF that they found themselves in a terrible state of being frozen, unable to move beyond it.

Both cases are examples of GREED.

St. Paul tells us that greed is idolatry. It is a least a sub-set of idolatry. When we are greedy we have put something that is NOT God before God. That is sin!

The Second Commandment tells to have no other gods besides Almighty God. When we value STUFF more than God, or put way too much value in STUFF, we are greedy and idolatrous.

God is not pleased when we put such high value on STUFF. All sorts of sins occur when we are trying to accumulate too much STUFF. We might end up stealing or cheating or lying to obtain the STUFF. We might be ruining our health or hurting others so that we get the STUFF we want.

The farmer didn't do that, did he? He came by his STUFF honestly. He probably worked hard to get his land to produce well.

But he was still lost in himself, looking after Ol' Number One only.

The end of the parable says:

[20]But God said to him, 'You fool! This very night your life is being demanded of you. And the things you have prepared, whose will they be?' [21]So it is with those who store up treasures for themselves but are not rich toward God."

Jesus' parable helps put things into

perspective. We see the end of the story, and it's not a pretty one. The Rich Fool is not going to enjoy the rest of his life in merriment and leisure. He had already reached the end of his days, and what did he have to show for them to God?

He hadn't already done all that merrymaking and taking at ease, not yet. Those activities were just in his mind. That was what he was planning to do.

His problem was that he had not already stored up treasure or riches toward God's account in his heart. That's all about how you spend your time and gifts each day.

Rather than building up an account for God, he was all about himself---thinking about himself, being good to himself. (That is very childish thinking.) There was nothing in the entire parable about his thinking beyond himself. He was truly a myopic thinker. His vision was all about doing what he felt like doing, about acquiring much STUFF for his own enjoyment.

The farmer, the Fool, found himself in a very new situation. His life was over, and he was about to stand before Almighty God in the Final Judgment.

This parable speaks loudly to us today: It's about greed. That's all about how we view STUFF.

We need to have a healthy attitude about our STUFF. We need to figure how we can appreciate and even enjoy our STUFF without making it a god. We cannot afford to let our STUFF cause us to be idolaters. God is not happy with us when we are idolatrous.

We need to see our STUFF as tools that allow us to do the jobs that God expects us to do.

The Fool didn't do well with the gift of time, either. He hadn't retired yet. (Remember the story took place on the eve before he retired.)

He didn't seem to have any plan for anyone else at all. His thoughts were only for himself. Part of what Jesus was telling us in that parable Is to caution us about our retirement. The farmer had no thought for anyone else. He was not looking around to see what his great, new fortune might be able to accomplish for anyone. He was only interested in pleasing himself.

I can hear a voice within that parable telling us that when we come to retirement we need to be aware of our community and those around us who can benefit from our experience and wisdom and our STUFF. Our retirement years, or days, ought NOT be confined to self-pleasing. That's something the world would like us to believe we should do, but it is nothing short of idolatry.

Then we have to think that the farmer's choice to live for himself was not a new idea for him. He apparently had no family, or at least the parable doesn't mention any. I would expect that his plans for his retirement looked a lot like what he had been doing already—looking out for himself.

Remember the Katrina victims? Some of them are still angry and unhappy and apparently stuck in their loss. Some still mourn their lost STUFF—their homes, their things, their pictures, their books, their clothes, etc. Some can't seem to move from that terrible moment of loss.

Not all who suffered loss during Katrina are stuck there. Surely many people who suffered from Katrina have picked up the pieces of their lives and have moved on to a new part of life … thankfully.

Those are the people who realized that God's gifts are still theirs, and there is life and hope beyond their losses.

Think about it. What had the gulf coast residents really lost?

They lost STUFF. BUT….

- They have their lives

- They have their health— physical and mental

- They have their faith

- They have their education

- They have their senses of humor

- They have their skills and abilities

- They have time in front of them to begin again, maybe even try something new; maybe do something better this time.

- They have their loved ones

- They could still work; there's plenty of jobs available to any who will work

- They have energy to pick up and go on again.

The parable ends with Jesus' comment, "So it is with those who store up treasures for themselves but are not rich toward God.'

Being rich toward God is the objective for us all--BEING RICH TOWARD GOD.

When we store up treasures on earth and make them so important to us, what have we gained? The important thing is to store up on this earth something that begins in our hearts. It is putting God first in our heart, which will cause us to put God first in our lives … in everything we do and say … in the way we use and spend all the STUFF that God has given us.

That is BEING RICH TOWARD GOD— learning to use God's gifts to benefit this world and not keep them to ourselves alone.

Luke 13: 1-9

13 There were some present at that very time who told him of the Galileans whose blood Pilate had mingled with their sacrifices. 2 And he answered them, "Do you think that these Galileans were worse sinners than all the other Galileans, because they suffered thus? 3 I tell you, No; but unless you repent you will all likewise perish. 4 Or those eighteen upon whom the tower in Siloam fell and killed them, do you think that they were worse offenders than all the others who dwelt in Jerusalem? 5 I tell you, No; but unless you repent you will all likewise perish."

6 And he told this parable: "A man had a fig tree planted in his vineyard; and he came seeking fruit on it and found none. 7 And he said to the vinedresser, 'Lo, these three years I have come seeking fruit on this fig tree, and I find none. Cut it down; why should it use up the ground? 8 And he answered him, 'Let it alone, sir, this year also, till I dig about it and put on manure. 9 And if it bears fruit next year, well and good; but if not, you can cut it down.'"

THE FIGGY TREE (a.k.a. A PARABLE)

I don't think I ever walk across a busy street without thinking of my grandmother. Grandma Bowman, my father's mother, was widowed when she was 60. She had been a Methodist pastor's wife for many years. She had raised her children, led the church in many ways—choir, SS, fellowships. She was well known for her hospitality. Grandma Bowman had just been visiting my Aunt Betty, who had just been married that summer. In fact, she had just returned from that visit and had gone to the beauty shop to get her hair done when she stepped off the curb and was hit by a car going 60 mph! She was killed instantly. Grandma never knew what hit her. She was just 64 years old. She was in great health. I was nine years old when she died, but I don't think I ever cross a busy street, even today, when I don't think about her ... and how she died.

Death like that is shocking! Anytime someone dies when there's no preparation for it, we are shocked. It's not supposed to happen that way ... but sometimes it does.

This morning's scripture starts with news like that. There had been news about a couple of shocking events that took the lives of many people. In one case a tower fell over on top of people; eighteen people died because of the tower.

The other event was even worse. Some people were making sacrifices to God; Pilate (the Roman governor) had the worshippers killed and then had their blood mixed with the blood of their sacrifices. It was a shock to the Jewish sensibility! Co- mingling the blood of the people with the blood of the sacrifices! It was indecent! Everyone was sickened just thinking about it.

Jesus knew what the people were thinking, so our lesson begins by Jesus asking the people, "Do you think that the people died because of their great wickedness? Had they been greater sinners than others?" Then Jesus told them that "No, it had nothing to do with their sins; they are the same as everyone else. Everyone needs to repent. Without repentance, we will all die."

Then Jesus told a story…a parable.

It seems there was once a vineyard owned by a wealthy landowner. In this vineyard stood a little fig tree. One day the landowner was walking across the vineyard, when he noticed that the little fig tree had no fruit. He called to his gardener and inquired about the fig tree. The gardener agreed that there was no fruit on the tree; in fact, the tree had never produced fruit, not in its three years of life. Well, the landowner was not happy. "Cut down the tree! It doesn't deserve to take up ground. It should be cut down and a new tree given that space to grow."

The gardener had compassion on the fig tree. He pleaded with the landowner. "Please, let the little tree live. Give it one more year. I promise I will do everything I can to encourage its growth and its fruiting. I will dig around its roots and give it water and special food. Please give the little tree one more chance! If by then it still doesn't produce any fruit, then I'll agree to cut it down."

What do you suppose the one thing has to do with

the other? What does the concern about people dying suddenly have to do with the parable of the fig tree?

Let's look more closely at the story Jesus told of the vineyard, the owner, the un-producing fig tree, and the gardener.

The story was a parable.

The landowner in the story was God. The landowner was the one who had the final say in all that goes on in the vineyard. The landowner was not pleased with the fig tree, because it did not produce any fruit. He condemned the tree to be cut down.

The tree had not produced therefore it should die.

We are the fig tree. (We are each a fig tree.) The fig tree belongs to the landowner, and we belong to God. We live in the vineyard that God had placed us in.

You might ask, 'What sort of fruit might we be expected to produce? There's lots of possibilities.

Children are fruit, of course, and we were commanded to 'be fruitful and multiply' in Genesis. But that's not the fruit that this parable is looking at.

We see 'fruit' mentioned in various ways in the New Testament –the fruit of the vine, the fruit of our labors…

Remember Jesus told the people that those who had died needed to repent. There's a clue.

John the Baptist speaks of bearing fruit worthy

of repentance. You can find his statement in both Matthew and Luke in verses 3:8 in both Gospels.

John says the same thing as Jesus does in the parable he told about the fig tree. "All the trees that don't produce fruit will be cut down and thrown into the fire'. John says, 'produce fruit worthy of repentance.'

I believe the fruit that is being spoken of is the fruit of repentance.

Repentance brings us close to God. We begin our journey toward God when we are repentant. The landowner wanted fruit from the fig tree, and God wants us to come to God.

The deal about repentance is that when we repent we find God. If we are full of ourselves, we can't be repentant. The two are mutually exclusive. The same as you can't physically be in two places at the same time, we can't be un-repentant and close to God at the same time.

When we are so full of ourselves, we are unrepentant, and there is no room for God to come into our lives.

Repentance is the first step toward having a relationship with God. And that's what God desires of us and for us.

Christ did the ultimate in putting himself aside to bring us to God. In his suffering and death, Christ did for us what we don't do---humiliate ourselves in order to come to God.

Why do you suppose we don't repent? What is it

that causes us not to produce the 'fruit of repentance'?

I can think of five things that might help us understand the troubles we have with repentance.

Pride

Self-righteousness

Unbelief

Foolishness

Anger

Pride is the first problem that causes us not to repent. The funny thing about pride is that somehow we have hard times recognizing pride in ourselves. It's much easier to see pride in others than it is in ourselves. Pride may actually be the whole problem—and all the other problems come from pride. But we'll take pride as the first for now.

Pride comes from our feeling about ourselves, that we are better than others. We think of ourselves as more deserving, more able, more intelligent, or beautiful or wealthy or better in some other ways. Pride considers self first. We have the right to be better. We deserve better than some others. We are entitled to act as we want to, after all don't we deserve it? (I can think of several commercials on

T.V. that speak to that weakness in us. We deserve that more expensive whatever.)

Pride is about putting ourselves above others. If God has placed God's image in every person and God doesn't respect one person above any other, then neither should we. When we consider ourselves better or more deserving than others, then we are also saying that we are more important than God, whose image is within other humans, too.

We are gravely wrong when we do that.

Maybe it's just one great subset of pride, but self-righteousness is another reason we don't repent. The self-righteous person is one who think he's good enough to begin with. This person doesn't see a problem that needs repenting. Self-righteous people are one's who have been successful in many ways in life. They have been good in school, and in business or sport. They were always chosen for the team when teams were picked in school. They made the grade.

They have a great deal of confidence in their own abilities, and they don't know that they need a savior. The problem with the self-righteous persons is that they can't admit that they are wrong or have done something far enough amiss to require a savior to save them. The self-righteous person Is the one who will say, "No thanks, I don't need Jesus; I don't need saving, I'm O.K, just as I am." That is the person that Jesus cannot help, because they deny him. They deny the trouble they are in, and they just walk away from him. That is the person I am very concerned about.

The next problem is the problem of unbelief. It really is the opposite of self-righteousness. The self- righteous person, remember, thinks he doesn't need a savior; he's not sinned enough to worry about it.

The unbeliever is one who is very aware of his sins. But he doesn't realize that Jesus can help … that he came to help exactly them. The unbeliever knows only too well how deeply she has fallen. She knows she is a sinner, but she doesn't know that there's any help for her. The unbeliever needs to learn that Jesus was not just a man, a good man, an interesting teacher and a gifted physician. The unbeliever needs to know that Jesus was God who came to live among us and suffer and die for us. The unbeliever needs to know that this God-Man was the only one who could save us, and he did. The unbeliever is one whose God is too small. He doesn't realize how great and grand and wonderful the Lord, Jesus Christ is. He doesn't know that he can trust Jesus to forgive him all his sins and more than his, all the sins of the world.

The unbeliever has trouble repenting because he fears his sins are bigger than Jesus.

The fourth way we fail to repent is because of foolishness. That may not seem all that bad. We think of foolishness as immature thinking. And it is. It is also often contrasted in the Bible with wisdom, which is Godly thinking. People who are foolish think too much as the world thinks, which is putting self first.

People who are foolish get caught in the many addictions of the world—alcohol, drugs, gambling, all that. They are so caught by the foolishness of their thinking that they cannot repent and begin their life of faith.

I have to say that the greatest mistakes I've ever made were in this area. I'm sure I'm not alone, either. Being a fool is not an excuse for not repenting.

The final reason I would point to that keeps us from repenting is Anger. Anger is something that we all feel in our lives. Some of us are more aware of our own anger than others, but we all do feel anger. And anger, in itself is not wrong. Anger is a feeling like hunger. We all experience hunger, and we all experience anger. The problem comes when we allow our anger to capture us and act out of anger.

Then anger has become the master. The Bible tells us to be angry but do not sin. Recognize your anger, deal with it, but don't let it eat you up or explode all over your world. When we do that, we drive a wedge between ourselves and God.

Those are not all the reasons we don't bear the fruit worthy of repentance, but those can keep us thinking about where we are now.

The last character in the parable is the gardener.

I didn't forget the gardener. The Gardener is Christ Jesus. He is the one who looked on the unrepentant fig tree and had compassion. He is the one who pleaded with the wealthy landowner to give the tree a chance, a second chance to bear fruit.

Jesus came to this world to do just that for each of us. He suffered and died for our sins, so that we could have a second chance, to get it right, to bear the fruit of repentance, and get on the journey of faith that leads to eternal life.

Several years ago Dave and I were driving to a Sunday afternoon concert to see Stephen and his orchestra play. The concert was a ways north of where we lived, so we took off on this beautiful spring day. The weather was clear, the cars were moving right along; we were in Germany so the Autobahn was pretty fast. Dave was driving; we were doing a flat 100 miles an hour, when suddenly right in front of us we saw many red lights and saw the cars jamming on their brakes to keep from colliding from the cars in front. There had been a terrible accident on the road, and because everyone was traveling so fast, many cars couldn't stop before they were in the middle of the mess. There had been a terrible pile up of cars and many injuries—probably some fatalities. The next two hours we were stuck on the Autobahn in a 'parking lot' as we watched the helicopters and the emergency vehicles move to the accident and do their grim work. All the time we sat praising and thanking God that we were just a little behind that pileup and that we were not dead. It was that close!

We realized middle at that moment that we are living on borrowed time. We could easily have been in the of that accident; it would have been all over for us then. (Sometimes we think, "Those things only happen to the other fellow—to people we don't know personally." But it happened to my Grandmother. How close does it have to be?)

We are all living on borrowed time. Jesus gave us the borrowed time. He is the gardener for our lives. He had pleaded with the Father for us. He has pleaded our case and provided us some borrowed time. The deal is, none of us knows how much time there is for each of us. Some of us may think we know how much time there is left. If we think we know, we probably know it's not very long. – what? Weeks, months, a year or two? That's not much.

Jesus bought us some time so that we can produce fruit of repentance. Just like the gardener in the parable, who begged the landowner for some more time—one more year—in which he could encourage the fig tree and give it nourishment and help to begin to produce the required fruit.

Jesus bought us time from the landowner—his Father—when he suffered and died for us on the cross. The time he bought for us is precious. The time he bought for us needs to be used very carefully. The time he bought for us better be productive. I don't know what the "or else" will mean in specifics. But I don't want to find out.

The good news that comes to us from this parable is that although we have been judged as sinful people, Christ has stepped in to speak up for us. He has convinced the judge to give us a little more time, maybe another year. In that time, he has promised to help us. He will nourish us and encourage us and guide us to produce the required fruit.

So, Jesus has given us a little time to get it right. He has found a way to help us grow the fruit that we need to produce. He has found a way to help us draw near to the father—to become his friend.

[end with song: The Savior Is Waiting to Enter Your Heart.]

Luke 13: 31-35

31 At that time, some Pharisees came up and said to Jesus, "Get away from here, because Herod wants to kill you." 32 But he said to them, "Go and tell that fox, 'Look, I am casting out demons and performing healings today and tomorrow, and on the third day I will complete my work. 33 Nevertheless I must go on my way today and tomorrow and the next day, because it is impossible that a prophet should be killed outside Jerusalem.' 34 O Jerusalem, Jerusalem, you who kill the prophets and stone those who are sent to you! How often I have longed to gather your children together as a hen gathers her chicks under her wings, but you would have none of

it! 35 Look, your house is forsaken! And I tell you, you will not see me until you say, 'Blessed is the one who comes in the name of the Lord

HIS WORK

Newsweek Magazine wrote a story about Mr. Paul Bremer, who is our man in Iraq, trying desperately to get much accomplished before the end of June, when the Iraqi people are to be on their own with a new government in place.

"Schedule, schedule, schedule—that's what I want," Bremer raps out. "I want benchmarks for the number of days. I need a chart of what tasks are falling behind. There are so many tasks. He's training Iraq's new police civil-defense force and army. He's creating village councils, an anticorruption agency and inspector-general offices. Hospitals, schools, and sewage lines. In all, an astonishing 17,500 projects so far.

Bremer works 16-18 hours/day. His goal: to build something lasting in Iraq.

Mr. Bremer is on a serious time crunch. The reason it's a time crunch is that he's dealing with a date that can't be changed and he wants to do the job right. It will make a big difference to millions of people if he does. He wants to set things up so that they can have a good government, good elections, good laws, safe places to live and be educated and work. He's very focused on his job.

That's a lot of work for Bremer. I hope he can do everything he wants to. It will be good for the Iraqi people. [Note: There are still big problems in Iraq.]

How about us? Do we find times when we are faced with a deadline? When we have need to make something happen by a certain time, or else? Surely every event in our lives doesn't have such an intense requirement to meet a certain date, but occasionally there are events that call us to muster every gift we have to make something happen.

I think Jesus was nearing that stage, too. He was counting the days … counting the days … today, tomorrow, and the third day. He had to have much on his mind. There were so many things to do, so much to teach, so many to heal. He had to be very focused on his purpose.

Let's step back a bit, and get the picture:

Jesus has been in ministry for a while. John would tell us that Jesus was in ministry for about three years all told, but Luke and the other synoptic writers (Matthew and Mark) pack Jesus' ministry into one year.

Whichever is the case Jesus has been doing ministry for a while. Most of the time he has been in the area of Galilee, not far from where he grew up.— in the towns and countryside around the Sea of Galilee.

Jesus had developed quite a reputation. He was deeply loved by some—his followers and many others who followed on a part time basis. Most of those were simple folks from those areas.

There were others who were not so happy with Jesus. Among those were the Jewish leadership—the lawyers, scribes, Pharisees and Sadducees. Each of those groups of men had different reasons to be concerned about Jesus.

Sometimes we think there was a simple division between those for and those against Jesus. The country folk were for Jesus; the better educated, city folk, those leaders of the Jews, did not like Jesus. He posed a problem to them. They feared him.

But it's not all that cut and dried. Jesus had supporters from many places. Even in among the Pharisees. Again, sometimes we think that there was always an uneasy relationship between Jesus and the Pharisees, but not every Pharisee was against Jesus. In our lesson today, that is certainly the case.

Some Pharisees came to Jesus to warn him; they feared for his life. They had discovered that King Herod was after Jesus, and they came to warn him to get out of Galilee, so he wouldn't be in Herod's jurisdiction.

But Jesus' response to the friendly Pharisees is a surprise. He told them, *Go tell that ol' fox what I'm doing.*

That ol' fox! Jesus was not using a kindly term on Herod. He knew the man for what he was—a blood-thirsty, evil man. But he did not fear him. Jesus didn't fear death from Herod. No, he knew there was work to be done, and it didn't involve Herod.

Jesus gave the Pharisees a message to take to Herod, "Tell him what I'm doing—performing cures and casting out demons." Jesus was fully engaged in the work that he had been given from his Father in Heaven, and he wasn't about to be swayed from it by a threat from Herod.

Jesus' words tell us that he was focused on the job to be done. He continued saying, 'Today, tomorrow, and the third day and my work is done.

Yes, today, tomorrow and the next day I'll be on my way to Jerusalem." There Jesus would face death.

Jesus sounds almost driven by his sense of timing, as he spoke to the Pharisees.

Jesus' mind was on his work, too. I don't know how many specifics he had in mind to do before the last day, but he certainly knew that time was a factor.

Jesus went on to say that he knew he would not die in Galilee. No, it is impossible for a prophet to die anywhere but in Jerusalem. That's where all the prophets had died at the hands of the Jews, their fellow Israelites. Many had come and died in Jerusalem.

Seems that Jesus takes that moment to sigh and lament over the Holy City. *"Jerusalem, O, Jerusalem, the city that kills the prophets and stones those who are sent to it. How often I have desired to gather your children together as a hen gathers her brood under her wings, and you were not willing!"*

According to Luke, Jesus had not yet traveled to Jerusalem, so perhaps it's better to see Jesus' words as those of his Father. God was lamenting the waywardness of the Jews. They were difficult children who would not come to God's care.

Jesus called the Jerusalemites, headstrong creatures. Chicks who refused to come under the wing of their mother hen.

Those in Jerusalem were the same as everywhere else. They were sinful. They were self- indulgent; greedy; boastful; lustful; untruthful; they didn't love God above all else, but put their petty desires ahead of everything else. They were prideful and arrogant. They were loose with their morals and tight with their gifts. They were a miserable bunch of people, yet Jesus was coming for them.

Jesus' work would not be done in Galilee. No, he knew his true "work" was yet ahead of him, and it couldn't happen except in Jerusalem.

Jesus had told his disciples earlier about his impending death, but he had not spoken publicly about dying until this time with the Pharisees.

In Luke chapter 9 and 51 it says that from that time, Jesus set his face to Jerusalem. Jesus had work to do in that city. He would not be turned from it.

Jesus was certainly in the middle of a time crunch. It's hard to imagine all that he had to do. He had to teach his disciples everything he wanted them to know about being disciples, about prayer and walking with God everyday. He had to be sure they understood his message and that they would be able to continue on when they were without him. How could he crowd all that into a few months? Or a few weeks or days that he had left?

Yesterday many of us went to the theater to see The Passion of the Christ. It was not an entertaining movie, but it was a vivid picture of what we know of Christ's suffering and death from the gospels. Different people walked away from that movie with different feelings. For me it was a vivid portrayal of the story I've studied. There were no surprises in it. There were a few additions, but not many, of the story. [Nothing of significance.] I believe, though, I did recognize more clearly the meaning of the suffering that Jesus experienced. I think we tend to focus on his dying for our sins, but his death actually relieved him of the suffering that he experienced before he died. It was a torturous suffering that was punishing and cruel and awful in its every moment, and Jesus allowed himself to endure it all because he wanted to, because he loves us. His suffering and death were his work. That's what the theologians have always called it. Christ's 'work' on the cross is what saves us.

Jesus came to heal us, each and everyone of us, from our sins and those things that keep us from being the person we can be, the child of God we are called to be. Jesus' healing includes physical healing. We've all experienced that—healing of the skinned knee and bruised shin; healing from a cold or flu or worse. Every time we experience healing it is God who heals. Jesus' healing includes healing of every kind—mental, emotional, relational, physical. And the greatest healing of all; it includes healing of our broken relationship with God.

We all need his healing, his salvation.

You met my Mom when she came here at Christmas. I want to share this email that she sent me last Wed:

"This has been a very busy day starting off with my Bible class here. That went very well and after lunch I picked up two other ladies and we went down to the hospital to visit two of our parishioners, one of whom is in our Bible group. She is terminal, I'm afraid. They are sending her home tomorrow with no hope. We were all devastated but tried to put on a brave face and then we prayed together ... that is ... I prayed. None of the others ever volunteer. The other patient they are sending home tomorrow to a wheel chair existence, I'm afraid. we have so many who are slipping in our congregation. After that we went back to Bertha's new home of assisted living and while walking down a hallway she stopped to say hello to a woman and then introduced us and she mentioned that I was their Bible teacher. This lady immediately turned to me with tears in her eyes and said she had lost faith in God. She had not been raised in a church, had married a man she didn't love but had children with him. Never went to church and now God won't forgive her!!! Well!!!! I felt that God put me there and that woman there at the same time so I could do something about that, but that is a big responsibility. I talked to her for 20 minutes before I had to leave, but I am going back tomorrow to talk to her again privately and to take her "The Message" to read. She has never had a Bible lesson or even ever read it so I think that book is a good one to start with. I will also take the Psalms.

Margie, I need help! I really feel, am certain about it as a matter of fact, that God put me there today for a reason and I can't fail Him. I wish I could take your course for the Lay Leader. Is there a book I can read about talking faith to someone.??? I did my best today but need Help! I think I have a very small calling for this and I want to improve any tiny talent that I have."

There it is. Every one of us needs Jesus in our lives. Every one of us needs his saving grace.

<u>FACNG THE END</u>

The day I began work at Wesley Seminary I could not even see the end. I was staring at 90 hours of graduate work ahead of me. Graduate work has a lot of teeth in it. There's much material to read, and I'm a slow reader. Every class you take requires a research paper usually between 15 and 20 pages long. The blue book exams are terrifying—so much to cram into the brain and then get down on paper.

Those ninety hours seemed like a long, black tunnel with no end to it. Going to seminary also would require my working at a church in another city, so I was on the road 5 to 6 days a week, putting a hundred miles on my car each day. I told Mother that by the time I got through this program I would be nearly 50 years old! So Mom said, "Yes, but you'll be fifty anyway."

That was what it was like facing the beginning of 3 ½ years of work. But what do we do when we are facing the end?

May 21st is the date of Stephen's graduation from high school, and I believe that Rebecca will graduate the first week of June.

I've noticed a certain change in Stephen recently. He's taking some serious courses this semester— Chem 2, Calculus and College prep English-- but he doesn't seem to be engaged heavily in the homework. There's a lighter attitude around the house. There's more playing, although he is still pretty busy with the youth projects that he's leading in town.

You might say that Stephen has a mild case of senioritis. He admits that it is so. It just seems harder for him to concentrate on the business of being in school.

Jesus was facing the end, the end of his ministry. He was confronted by some people who recognized the danger he was facing and warned him about it. Luke writes: *31At that very hour some Pharisees came and said to him, "Get away from here, for Herod wants to kill you."*

32Jesus replied, "Go and tell that fox for me, 'Listen, I am casting out demons and performing cures today and tomorrow, and on the third day I finish my work. 33Yet today, tomorrow, and the next day I must be on my way, because it is impossible for a prophet to be killed outside of Jerusalem.

Perhaps we can remember back to that time before graduation, that light feeling that it really didn't matter how hard we worked. We would pass; we would get our diplomas. Who would ask later about our GPA after all was said and done? We can laugh at senioritis, remembering that lazy, free feeling that lasted a few weeks. There may be other times in our lives when we experience that same feeling, but I'd like to suggest that there are some areas of life where we really must not have senioritis. That time is when we are facing the end.

We've all heard that today is the first day of the rest of our lives. So we can think that today we are facing the end.

This morning we're going to look at how we should face the end, what our attitude and actions must be. We shall begin by seeing how Jesus faced his last days, and then we'll turn to consider what he wants us do, how we should be living in these last days. We'll hear about Jesus' encounter with the friendly Pharisees, and then we'll look at our own responses. In this scripture Jesus gives us a perfect example of what it means to be of one purpose, to set our faces to a certain direction and not be dissuaded from it.

Some of the characters in this lesson are a bit of a surprise-the Pharisees who came to Jesus and warned him about Herod's deadly intentions. They are a surprise. Pharisees always seem to be in the opposition camp when we read about them in the Gospels. We read of many encounters between Jesus and the Pharisees and they are nearly always strained. The Pharisees are trying to catch Jesus in saying something against the Law, or they are complaining that Jesus has acted on the Sabbath to heal someone.

But in this encounter, we learn that there were some Pharisees that were not antagonistic to Jesus, in fact, they were seeking his safety. They might have been followers of Jesus. I believe we could count Nicodemus, the Pharisee who came to Jesus at night to speak with him, to be among the followers of Jesus.

Herod, whom Jesus calls "That Fox," was known to be sneaky and dangerous. And we know that Herod had taken John the Baptist prisoner and then later beheaded him. Herod was to be watched out for. Herod was a very wicked man. Herod might destroy Jesus, as he had Jesus' cousin, John.

But this warning didn't bring the expected response. Jesus didn't change his plans. He was not particularly concerned about Herod. Jesus knew that his destination was Jerusalem and that he would die there, so Herod was not an issue.

Prior to this scripture, Luke told us that Jesus set his face to go to Jerusalem. This happened following his transfiguration. Jesus turned at this point in his ministry toward Jerusalem, his final destination, and at that point Jesus set his face as well as his mind to pursue that goal.

Jerusalem was the end of the course for Jesus.

He knew that. Jesus told the Pharisees that Jerusalem is where he would die.

Jesus prophesied about his death several times before to his Apostles. But here Jesus is speaking rather openly to these Pharisees about it. Jesus said it is impossible for a prophet to die outside of Jerusalem. Remember, the Sanhedrin, the Jews' ruling body, met in Jerusalem, and they were the only legal body that could judge a person to be a prophet or a false prophet. Jesus knew he would stand trial before them soon.

Jesus knew there was danger about; he knew

his end was near and that he had little time left to attend to the work of his ministry, but Jesus remained faithful to his work to the end.

Jesus' example is perfect for us. He shows us how to set our faces to the end.

Our lives as Christians are a process of growing. We are not perfect in faith when we begin our life with Christ, but we are expected to grow in love and obedience and trust. We must depend on God's grace and the strength of the Holy Spirit to do this.

St. Paul once likened the Christian life to a foot race. Paul suggested that each of us needs to think of ourselves as being in a race, and that we are in the race to win it. In other words, we need to run all out, to put everything into our Christian life that we can find the strength to.

In our own Christian walk we may find ourselves tempted to slack up, to get off the track, to get distracted, or to wander away. That is not the example we are getting from Jesus. He has called us to do the best that we can.

In John Wesley's day there were people who would say, "If I have been saved by Grace through faith, then it doesn't matter what I do, because my faith is enough to get me into heaven." Wesley said that was foolish thinking, because that idea lulls a person into a false sense of security. God wants our active involvement in his kingdom and our fellowship with him.

Stacking arms is an expression within Army circles. It means a person who is soon to rotate into a new job or to retire simply stops doing his job, he stacks his arms (his guns) in the corner, so to speak, and just waits for his time to be accomplished.

Stacking arms is not called for in the Christian life.

Remaining faithful to our calling, leaning into the job, is also a command for the church. We, as a body of believers, need to continue to work together to be part of the body of Christ here in Stevenson.

Do you wonder what it is we're supposed to be doing? Before Jesus left the disciples on the mount in Galilee, he left them with marching orders—we call it the Great Commission. Jesus' orders were to make disciples, baptize them and teach them his commands.

That's pretty simple—three things:

Make disciples, welcome them into God's family (which is baptizing them), and help them to grow in their faith—teaching them.

From this scripture we know that we are not excused from this requirement, none of us are. I believe that as long as God gives us strength, we need to be about God's business—the business that he called us to do.

There was a remarkable woman at MMUMC where I worked, who was blind and confined to her home, yet she had a great ministry of outreach to many people in her town just by talking to them on the phone. Nancy may have been disabled, but that did not deter her from doing what she could to further God's kingdom on earth. She faced her days doing God's .

I hope many of you saw Steven Spielberg's film Schindler's List. It came out in the early 90's. It is the true story of Oskar Schindler, a Nazi businessman during the War. He was a great opportunist who saw a way to make a great deal of money because of the war. He was in business to make himself very rich.

He enjoyed the finest things—fine wine, women, clothes, cars. He also enjoyed his Nazi connections that brought him into social circles that he wanted.

Schindler employed Jewish prisoners as laborers in his factory; the labor was very cheap, and he made a huge amount of money. Gradually, Schindler began to see the real horror of the death camps; he saw the devastation of the Warsaw ghetto, when all the Jews were either murdered or taken to prison camp. He saw the fallout from the ovens that burned Jews. He saw much of the horror that was going on at the death camps, and something inside him changed. Something inside Schindler said, "Enough of this! This is wrong. Whatever I can do to save these people, I will do."

It was in the last year of the war, and the extermination of the Jewish race was gathering speed. Schindler began racing against time to buy Jews to save them from being murdered. He began compiling lists of Jews that had worked for him, couples, families, and he began to negotiate with the Nazis to buy them.

The price was great, and it cost him a much. Then, on top of the ransom he paid for the people, Schindler had to feed these people for nearly a year.

At the end of the war, Schindler was acting as a man possessed with one thought—he was using every Pfennig he had and every connection he could make to free another and then another human from certain death.

At the end of the war, Schindler had become penniless, but he had secured the freedom of 1100 Jews. The epilog of the movie tells us that there are 4000 Jews living in Poland today, but the descendants of Schindler's Jews number 6000.

I have seen no better example today of facing the end than Oskar Shindler's. He saw an end coming—the end of these people, and he saw that he might be part of a solution for saving some of them.

To that end Schindler put his entire fortune. He would not rest until he had rescued every person that he could.

On commentator said that Schindler's life goes to show the good in all humanity, but I beg to differ. I think Oskar Schindler began hearing God's voice, God's command, to make a difference in his world.

He was responding to God's call.

Schindler's earlier life certainly didn't give evidence of his walking in faith with Christ, but finally Oskar Schindler realized what was happening, and he responded; he gave to his last penny; he gave life to a thousand people, and he gave us a wonderful example of how to face the end.

Luke 15: 1-7

15 ¹² *Now all the tax-collectors and "outsiders" were crowding around to hear what he had to say. The Pharisees and the scribes complained of this, remarking, "This man accepts sinners and even eats his meals with them."*

³⁻⁷ *So Jesus spoke to them, using this parable: "Wouldn't any man among you who owned a hundred sheep, and lost one of them, leave the ninety-nine to themselves in the open, and go after the one which is lost until he finds it? And when he has found it, he will put it on his shoulders with great joy, and as soon as he gets home, he will call his friends and neighbours together. 'Come and celebrate with me,' he will say, 'for I have found that sheep of mine which was lost.' I tell you that it is the same in Heaven— there is more joy over one sinner whose heart is changed than over ninety-nine righteous people who have no need for repentance.*

WELCOMING JESUS

Many years ago, when we lived in Izmir, Turkey, Dave and I had an opportunity to spend an overnight with two couples we knew from our chapel group. One of the wives was a Turkish woman named Belma. We were all going to drive to her home town in order to look at a place on a lake where they might want to rent for the summer. Both of the other couples had little children, and they were thinking it might be good to take the children to the lake for the summer.

We planned to drive out to the little village Friday night, eat dinner at the Belma's aunt's home, spend the night there, and look around the next day to think about the summer possibilities. We would drive back to town Saturday night.

So we drove out to the village and arrived at Belma's aunt's home. We were ushered into the parlor, a nice room that was closed off from all the other rooms in the house. We waited in that room for a while. (I was hungry. I was expecting Leslie, so I liked being fed close to dinner time.) We continued to wait. Belma's aunt came into the room and spoke to her niece about something. Then the aunt left and we waited … and waited … and waited. Finally, the aunt came in, again. She again spoke to her niece, and then the niece spoke to her husband, and he announced to us all (in English) that we would be going out for dinner!!

It seems that the aunt knew we were coming for dinner, and she had prepared a nice meal for us, but they had surprise visitors, who arrived before we did. And the host family fed our dinner to the guests!

Our subject today is welcoming.

Our message this morning comes from one word that is part of the setting of the passage in Luke 15. Most passages include a setting, telling the reader the context of the passage. It's good to note the setting, but I don't usually think of getting the big message in that spot.

But as I read and reread the first verse of Luke's words for today, I could hear one word telling me to slow down, in fact, "Stop!"

The Pharisees and the Scribes were upset with Jesus because they didn't like that he associated with the wrong sort of people. The Jews had a saying: "Bad company corrupts good character." So they didn't like Jesus welcoming the tax collectors and sinners. They didn't like people who ran around with the riff raff.

The Jews believed that they were the only acceptable people in the world. All the people in the world, except for the children of Abraham, were NOT

O.K. They were unclean. The Jews couldn't be in their company: not in their homes; not eating with them. If it was necessary to do business with gentiles, so be it, but DON"T go into their homes or spend unnecessary time with them.

(Remember how the Jewish leaders stood outside Pilate's headquarters and called up to him when they wanted Jesus condemned to death by the Romans? They didn't want to defile themselves by stepping foot into a gentile place on the eve of Passover. That would have made them ritually unclean, and then they would have not been able to eat the Passover Seder with their families that night.

Then within the Jewish community there were low-lifes—the tax collectors who had aligned themselves with Rome. They were working directly for Rome, exacting taxes from everyone, and keeping more than was required by Rome for themselves.

They were legalized pirates. Nobody liked tax collectors.

The Pharisees also hated those who failed morally and those who didn't keep themselves ritually clean. If you worked outside or worked with your hands, the Pharisees would have considered you a 'sinner'.

Today we have our own categories of people who are NOT okay for polite society. We know who they are.

They are people we have spent time keeping our kids from associating with. After all, we too, are known for the company we keep. We may have gone to great measures to be sure our children are not friends with certain people. Maybe we even picked out friends for our children to spend time with.

And the same rules apply to us. We steer clear of certain places and groups. Right? (I remember when I was knocking on doors in this neighborhood when I first came here. I was cautioned by one neighbor not to knock on the door of the house across the street from her, because it was a 'shot house'. Actually, I had already been there and spoken to a man with a hook instead of a hand. But if I had known it was dangerous, I probably would have walked on by.)

That's what the Pharisees and the scribes were saying about Jesus. He spent time and even ate with the wrong sort of folks. If he was so close to them, he certainly couldn't be any good himself. Look at the company he kept!

But think about it: The reason for such rules is to protect us so we are not influenced to do bad things ourselves. We don't need to be picking up bad habits from others. We don't need the trouble those folks might bring us.

The more I thought about it, I began to realize that welcoming wasn't just something that Jesus did on a couple of occasions. NO! Welcoming was exactly what Jesus was all about. He came to welcome people, all sorts of people, and especially sinners, to him.

What is welcoming anyway?

Welcoming is being hospitable to others. We are trained to show hospitality to others, especially people near us, people like us. But true hospitality goes beyond those who can return the favor.

Hospitality is making another welcome into our life and space. Even if we are not home or in our own surroundings, we can still be hospitable by welcoming another into our midst; being interested in the other; giving the gift of presence—that is being wholly available to that person rather than having other things on our mind. Being welcoming is the first step in making a friend.

Jesus welcomed tax gatherers and sinners.

Remember Jesus came to earth with a mission. He came to save the lost. He came to invite us to come with him into the kingdom of God. He came to welcome us, and everyone who would listen to him, to join Him and His Heavenly Father.

So of course Jesus went to those who were going the wrong way.

Jesus wasn't about to be changed by those people. We saw that when Jesus went into the wilderness and fasted for forty days. Jesus met the Devil there; he was tempted three times by the Devil, and he did not succumb. If Jesus didn't fall to temptation when being directly assaulted by the Devil, don't think he would have been corrupted by spending time with socially unfavorable characters.

Jesus came to call everyone in order to get some to follow. Jesus' rubbing elbows with those folks, even eating with them, wasn't going to change him. He was all about changing those he called. He wanted them to change to HIS way—the Kingdom Way. The Jewish leadership didn't understand that. So Jesus told them parables. The parables were about those who were lost and what the owner does to find them.

This morning we'll look at the first parable.
Jesus began by asking a question.

Which of you, having a hundred fold of sheep and losing one, would not leave the ninety-nine to themselves, and go in search of the one? Who of you would not search for and wide to find the missing sheep? Who would not place that sheep on his shoulders and carry him carefully all the way home when he was found? Who of you would not?

Certainly you can understand the love the shepherd felt for his lost sheep. Certainly you can imagine the shepherd expending much energy looking for the lost one. Can you not imagine the relief and the joy the shepherd would feel when the lost was finally found? Can you not imagine the shepherd calling his family and friends to share in his joy--to come to a fiesta celebrating the return of the one who has been found and restored to the flock?

Can you not imagine?

Jesus asked the question leading his audience to participate with the sheep owner in his efforts to find what he lost. After all, the sheep belonged to him. He loved his sheep, and he would do whatever was necessary to gain him back.

Jesus continued: "I tell you, in the same way there will be more rejoicing in heaven over one sinner who repents than over ninety-nine righteous persons who do not need to repent."

That parable and Jesus' comments following tell us exactly what Jesus' purpose on earth was—to seek out the lost and lead them to repent.

TO SEEK OUT THE LOST AND LEAD THEM TO REPENT.

I think we understand that at some point we were all lost sheep. We all needed to be found by Jesus and brought to the fold. We know that in this world there are no righteous people: *"For all have sinned and fallen short of the glory of God."* (Rom 3:23)

We all start out lost, but Jesus is seeking us, reaching out to us, calling our names, and rejoicing when we are found.

So the sheep in the fold are those who have been found by Jesus, who know his voice and who have come to him and follow him. We are the sheep of his pasture.

There are some of us who grew up in the fold. We grew up in the church and have been following Jesus, our shepherd. I am sometimes concerned that we don't quite know how much we have—being part of the flock. We may be naïve about how life would be on the outside.

On the other hand, there are some of us who have been part of the flock, but we managed to slip away and found ourselves very lost in some terrible way. It would involve lying to the world, indulging in some wrong.

Whatever the wrong, did the Savior come find you? Did you repent and find his willing and welcoming arms open to you? Did you realize how very great the day you were found was to you? Did you realize how much the angels in heaven rejoiced when you were found?

I give thanks every day to God for that time. I give thanks, not for my failure, but for the lessons that I learned and the gifts I now have. I give thanks and rejoice in my deepest being that Christ came looking for me and carried me back to the fold to grow in him.

Jesus went out in search of the lost. That story he told the Pharisees was all about himself. He has come into the far country, seeking to befriend the lost and to make them his own, saying, "*Come unto me all ye who labor and are heavy laden, and I will give you rest.*" (Matt 11:28)

Jesus came to call the lost, and today we see him calling the lost in two ways: through the activity of the Holy Spirit, and through us Christians, who were first found of Jesus and are now following him.

I believe there is a word for us in this scripture today. The word is WELCOMING. If we have the mind of Christ, then our actions should be doing what Jesus did. Jesus came to welcome all he met, especially those who were lost from the fold.

We need to carry a welcoming presence with us to all we meet. St. Paul wrote that *"he would be all things to all people so that he might win some of them to Christ."* In other words, Paul went into many situations and met people, made them welcome in his presence, learned of them, spoke to them of their condition, and shared Christ with them.

We may be finding that our days as parents of small children have long been over. Our influence on our own families has dwindled and belongs to our children to raise up the next crop of young people, but there are many people we can meet today who don't know Christ, or who might have been part of a flock, a community, at one time, but they have strayed and gotten lost. They need to be found. If we are welcoming in our attitude to those we meet, and we make new friends, we can lead them to our fellowship where they can grow in the LORD.

Luke 15: 11-32

11-19 *Then he continued, "Once there was a man who had two sons. The younger one said to his father, 'Father, give me my share of the property that will come to me.' So he divided up his property between the two of them. Before very long, the younger son collected all his belongings and went off to a foreign land, where he squandered his wealth in the wildest extravagance. And when he had run through all his money, a terrible famine arose in that country, and he began to feel the pinch. Then he went and hired himself out to one of the citizens of that country who sent him out into the fields to feed the pigs. He got to the point of longing to stuff himself with the food the pigs were eating and not a soul gave him anything. Then he came to his senses and cried aloud, 'Why, dozens of my father's hired men have got more food than they can eat and here I am dying of hunger! I will get up and go back to my* father, and I will say to him, "Father, I have done wrong in the sight of Heaven and in your eyes. I don't deserve to be called your son any more. Please take me on as one of your hired men.'"

20-24 So he got up and went to his father. But while he was still some distance off, his father saw him and his heart went out to him, and he ran and fell on his neck and kissed him. But his son said, 'Father, I have done wrong in the sight of Heaven and in your eyes. I don't deserve to be called your son any more ....' 'Hurry!' called out his father to the servants, 'fetch the best clothes and put them on him! Put a ring on his finger and shoes on his feet, and get that calf we've fattened and kill it, and we will have a feast and a celebration! For this is my son—I thought he was dead, and he's alive again. I thought I had lost him, and he's found!' And they began to get the festivities going.

25-32 "But his elder son was out in the fields, and as he came near the house, he heard music and dancing. So he called one of the servants across to him and enquired what was the meaning of it all. 'Your brother has arrived, and your father has killed the calf we fattened because he has got him home again safe and sound,' was the reply. But he was furious and refused to go inside the house. So his father came outside and called him. Then he burst out, 'Look, how many years have I slaved for you and never disobeyed a single order of yours, and yet you have never given me so much as a young goat, so that I could give my friends a dinner?

But when that son of yours arrives, who has spent all your money on prostitutes, for him you kill the calf we've fattened!' But the father replied, 'My dear son, you have been with me all the time and everything I have is yours. But we had to celebrate and show our joy. For this is your brother; I thought he was dead— and he's alive. I thought he was lost— and he is found!'"

Luke 15: 11-32

<u>REMEMBERING WHO YOU ARE</u>

Happy Father's Day! I'm not a father. I suppose over the years we've heard more Father's Day messages (and Mother's Day messages) from fathers than we have from mothers.

I'd like to begin by telling you about my father, Dave Bowman. You met Daddy when he and Mama came to Highlands last Christmas. Daddy comes from Methodist stock … a long way back.

In fact Daddy's got a great-grandfather, Rev. Isaac Newton McAbee, who was a Methodist circuit rider in Western Pennsylvania and Ohio back in the 1800's. And Daddy's father was a Methodist pastor in the Pacific Northwest. So Daddy grew up in parsonages, and he knew about going to church on Sunday. That's the thing you do; that's part of who you are. You go to church, and you give thanks to God, and you worship God. You also go to Sunday school and youth group and everything else that the church has to offer.

Daddy knew. Then Daddy married Mama, and we started coming along. Daddy must have realized that three little girls might need some encouragement to get ready for church, so he ALWAYS began Sunday morning very early. Daddy would get up and turn on music on the high fi. He'd play <u>Tchaikovsky's 1812 Overture</u> or <u>Beyond the Blue Horizon</u> or whatever he had that made great noise. He'd turn on the music FULL VOLUME, and THEN he'd march around to our bedrooms telling us to get up. He'd pick up the stuffed animals and pelt our beds with them … if we didn't jump out of bed.

THEN Daddy would go into the kitchen, and he would make homemade muffins for us. After that we'd get all dressed up and somehow fit into the car. I'm sure I can attribute me initial involvement with church, and the Methodist Church, to my Daddy. You could say that my Daddy helped me to begin to understand who I am as a child of God.

Some young people look forward to the day when they will leave home. Sometimes that will be going away to college or to take a job in a new community. Sometimes those occasions bring on trouble, though, because the young person finds himself on his own for the first time in life. Suddenly every decision he makes is completely his own. In the new community there is nobody who knows him, and the young person has a freedom he never had before. Sometimes the decisions she makes aren't so good. The crowd they choose to hang around with might not be the best choice. They may discover new activities that are unhealthy. They seem to have forgotten who they were before they left home.

Jesus told a parable about a man who had two sons. The father's wealth was very, very great. He had enormous holdings. One day the younger son came to his father and asked, "Could he please have whatever was his fair share of the estate, so that he could take it with him and go into the world and do his thing?" The father agreed to give the young man his share, and very soon the fellow found himself off on his way to a new life.

The glitz and glamour of the big city lured him, so he followed his inclination and traveled many miles to it. As he made his way into the busy streets, his eyes caught many sights that he had not seen at home. He saw people dressed in grand finery. He thought his own simple dress was inferior to the silks and satins and lush colors and rich brocades he saw on these city people. The first days the young man visited the tailor and had a fine wardrobe made just for him. He was filled with awe at his new self as he paraded around the town in his new clothes.

The young man discovered a gambling place, and he learned to gamble. While he was playing, he found new friends who were very happy to join his company, especially as he was paying for everyone's way. The young man discovered women. He spent a great deal of money on them.

The young man had made a reputation for being a big spender. He paid much for the games, for banquets, for women, for his ever-new costumes. It didn't take long for the young man to develop another habit, along with the gaming and the women. He began drinking. The drinking habit kept him from feeling pain of his gambling losses. The young man began to drink more and more, and as he drank, his thinking became foggy. He made more bad choices.

Times were beginning to change, too. People were getting nervous about the news of the crops failing. There was talk of famine and people were worried. The young man didn't have such a fat pocket now, but he still had all his beautiful clothes and his home.

The day came when the young man lost really big. He lost more than he could pay. He knew that last bet was more than he could cover, but he tried to tell himself that he would win, and winning would make all the difference. But the dice rolled; his chips were taken, and he was shocked. He was deeply in debt. He turned over the deed to his place, including everything he owned in the place. In a matter of a few days the young man had gambled away the last of his belongings. He was very drunk, so he wasn't even much aware of the mess he was in.

The friends he thought were so good, vanished when his funds were gone, and he was completely alone. He didn't know what to do. His pockets were empty; his fine clothes were no more; his friends he left; his mind was clouded with alcohol. He had nowhere to go.

Then he thought of the owner of a farm on the outside of town. He went there and hired himself out to the man to feed the man's pigs. The young man was still very fuzzy in his mind; at first he thought he was dreaming everything that had happened— losing the games, his money, his place, his friends. Going to the farm and feeding the pigs---that had to be a dream. Pigs were disgusting, unclean, and filthy. The law even forbade him to touch a pig. Yet he was hungry, and the slop he was feeding the pigs looked pretty good to him.

The young man did not leave home with the intention of making a terrible mess of his life. He left, taking along his inheritance, looking to better himself, to make his fortune. But problems came. He made bad decisions. He had forgotten who he was!

In that way the young man's story could be ours. In our world we are hardly exempt from mistakes.

How many of us have been given gifts only to squander them? Gifts like time, education, health, family, talents, and resources?

We seem to spend our lives squandering our gifts. Sometimes we just fritter away gifts— wasting time, fooling around in school, throwing money away on the lottery. Sometimes we develop bad habits like smoking or drinking or eating the wrong foods. Some of us never get out and exercise, so we are squandering the good health we've been given by not treating our bodies right. Each of us has been given precious talents, but we have let these gifts wither away. What a shame that any of our gifts be squandered.

The best gift may be the hardest to describe.

That would be our relationship with our LORD. That is a gift, one he gives us when we come to him. That gift must be cultivated, like any good friendship. We have to spend time with Jesus our friend If we want to feel close to him. We have to begin to understand how he thinks and how he wants us to live in this world he has given us. That takes time to read his Word and to spend time in prayer listening for him to speak to us.

We squander that gift when we fill our lives full of distractions. We can't go into a room without snapping on the T.V. or the radio. We have to be reading something or talking on the phone … or doing something. When do we ever listen to Him? I don't want to suggest that those activities are wrong. They are not. But NEVER taking time to be with the LORD has the result of starving us spiritually. Do you suppose we are living as if we've forgotten who we are as Children of God?

I'd like to tell you a story about Henry Martyn Childs. Henry was a young man living in Montreal in the 19th Century. He came from a family with seven sons. Henry was one of the middle sons. Henry's father was a very successful merchant in Montreal. Henry attended a private school for several years, but when he reached sixteen, he ran away. He ran away to find gold in Nevada, but after only a little while he lost all his money. Then Henry became lost in the desert with another man. The other man eventually lost his mind, which frightened Henry considerably.

Finally, the two were found, and Henry made his way to San Francisco. Henry found a ship heading to England, and he signed on as a seaman in a sailing vessel. Life at sea was severe. They weathered many storms, and Henry, being the smallest seaman aboard, had to climb to the top of the mast whenever the skipper needed someone up there.

The ship sailed around the Horn, and ultimately it landed in Liverpool. Henry had squandered many gifts and forgotten who he was.

Back at the farm the young man finally began to think clearly. The mental fog, which had enveloped his mind for so long, had lifted, and he knew things were bad. The gnawing pain in his stomach was screaming for attention. He was hungry, and he needed food; and he needed more than that.

They young man had had no drink either, and gradually, as he dried out, he began to think straight; he came to his senses. A thought came to him. "I am in a really bad place here, but at my father's home, even his servants get fed every day. They are not starving.

So the young man thought, "I shall return home and beg my father for a position like the least of his servants."

He pulled himself up from the mud and began the journey home. The journey was long, but he pressed on. He even enjoyed the spring rain that showered him all over, washing away the mud from his torn rags. By now his sandals were worn out and hardly gave any protection from the rocks on the road.

As he made his way home, he envisioned how it might be when he arrived home. He hoped that he would be able to speak to his father. He knew how things were when he left the house. He had been so headstrong and so determined when he left home that he had not noticed the tears in the corners of his father's eyes. He had not noticed the shock on his brother's face.

He had practiced what he would say to his dad.

He knew by now that he had really screwed his life up. He had taken the great wealth that he had been given and squandered it. On what? On terrible things. His dad would want an accounting of his dealings, and the young man didn't even want to think about all that. He really wanted to forget that whole miserable episode.

He finally settled on a simple, humble statement that he could say to his dad. Then the chips could fall where they may. *"I will say to him, 'Father, I have sinned against heaven and before you; I am no longer worthy to be called your son; treat me like one of your hired hands.'"*

As he was yet far down the road the father spied his son approaching and ran out to him. The father had not moved so quickly in some time, but he ran full out to his approaching child. When he reached his son, the father encircled his son with his strong arms and gave his son a great bear hug. Then he kissed the boy with great delight on each cheek. The father stepped back a moment and surveyed his son. He was thrilled to see him again. His son was back. He remembered! He remembered who he was and where his home was and where his father was!

The boy began to repeat his oft-practiced lines: *"Father I have sinned against heaven and before you; I am no longer worthy to be called your son...."*

The father didn't even listen to the rest of his son's words, rather he called his servants, saying, "*quickly, get a robe for my son, the finest in the house, and bring a ring for his finger and sandals for his feet. Then send orders for the fatted calf to be prepared. We shall have a feast today! We shall surely celebrate, for this son of mine was dead but is now alive; he was lost, but has been found.*"

The moment the son saw his dad he was thrilled to be home. He shared the thrill of reuniting with his father, being home safe and sound. The fine robe, the dazzling ring, the new Nikes on his feet meant little compared to the wonder of being gathered into his dad's loving arms, to hear his father tell the whole household how his son, who had been dead, was now alive.

The son was home again. He had been restored to the family, having all the rights and privileges that he had walked away from before. He was also filled with the most wonderful feeling of love and joy.

Remember Henry? We left him in Liverpool. He had literally been around the world and was far from home. It had been a very long time since he had stepped into his home; sat at the family table with his six brothers and his dad and mother. He was so far from home. So far from anyone who cared about him.

But when the ship docked in Liverpool, a man standing on the boardwalk was heard calling up to anyone on board, "Is Henry Martyn Childs aboard?"

Someone on deck heard his voice and hollered back to the man, "He's here on this ship."

The man on the boardwalk worked at the YMCA in Liverpool; he came on board the ship and found Henry.

It seems that George Childs, the boy's father, had been searching for his son, and he had contacted the YMCA in Liverpool, thinking that Henry might be on a ship porting there.

When the YMCA man found Henry, he took him off the ship, as per instructions from his father. Henry was cleaned up, given clothes befitting a young gentleman and sent back to Montreal on a first class ticket. By this time Henry was quite ready to accept such accommodations.

When he returned home his father told him, "Remember that you are the son of a gentleman. If you want to travel, do so as a gentleman."

I don't suppose any of you have ever heard this story before, but it's a true story. Henry Martyn Childs was my mother's grandfather—my great-grandfather. That story has been passed down to each generation in my family.

The story of the son could be our story. To some degree each of us has had or will have a time when we make the wrong choices and find ourselves in a bad situation.

We humans are not like other animals who live by instinct, who are 'programmed' to live a certain way. We have choices and have to learn to make good choices.

The story is often called the story of the Prodigal

Son, but that is a misnomer. The son is called prodigal because he squanders all the resources on lavish living. But the original meaning of the story was to call the father the 'prodigal'. The word prodigal means one who is lavish in spending. It truly is the Father who is the prodigal in the story. The son had used up all the resources given to him by his Father, yet the Father continued to lavish gifts on the son when he returned.

That's the way it is with our heavenly Father. God is lavish in his giving to us even when we have already squandered so much of his love; even though we have made a mockery of his calling us. Even though we have acted like we didn't know the right from the wrong, the Father is calling to us; waiting for us to turn to him and return to him.

Can you picture the Father, eyes searching the horizon for signs of our return?

Can you imagine His yearning for us to come back to him?

Do you realize how deeply he wants each one of us to come home?

When we come to our senses and remember who we are and return to our Father, we are always restored beyond our wildest dreams.

Remember Jesus' words? "I tell you there will be more joy in heaven over one sinner who repents than over ninety-nine righteous persons who need no repentance."   AMEN.

¹⁹ "Now there was a rich man, and he habitually dressed in purple and fine linen, joyously living in splendor every day. ²⁰ And a poor man named Lazarus was laid at his gate, covered with sores, ²¹ and longing to be fed with the *crumbs* which were falling from the rich man's table; besides, even the dogs were coming and licking his sores. ²² Now the poor man died and was carried away by the angels to Abraham's bosom; and the rich man also died and was buried. ²³ In Hades he lifted up his eyes, being in torment, and *saw Abraham far away and Lazarus in his bosom. ²⁴ And he cried out and said, 'Father Abraham, have mercy on me, and send Lazarus so that he may dip the tip of his finger in water and cool off my tongue, for I am in agony in this flame.' ²⁵ But Abraham said, 'Child, remember that during your life you received your good things, and likewise Lazarus bad things; but now he is being comforted here, and you are in agony. ²⁶ And ⁽ˡ⁾besides all this, between

us and you there is a great chasm fixed, so that those who wish to come over from here to you will not be able, and *that* none may cross over from there to us.' ²⁷ And he said, 'Then I beg you, father, that you send him to my father's house— ²⁸ for I have five brothers—in order that he may warn them, so that they will not also come to this place of torment.' ²⁹ But Abraham *said, 'They have Moses and the Prophets; let them hear them.' ³⁰ But he said, 'No, father Abraham, but if someone goes to them from the dead, they will repent!' ³¹ But he said to him, 'If they do not listen to Moses and the Prophets, they will not be persuaded even if someone rises from the dead.'"

CONVINCED!

Remember the story that starts out, 'Marley was dead, to begin with. There is no doubt whatever about that'? I expect some of you do. That's the way Dickens began his tale <u>A Christmas Carol</u>. It was Ebenezer Scrooge, Marley's business partner, who thought about Marley being dead. Scrooge and Marley had not been just associates; they had been two of a kind—brothers in the world of commerce, pinching every penny all the way to the bank.

Scrooge outlasted Marley and continued on in business, doing as they had always done—making much money. **Scrooge was convinced** that his success in business was because of his fine business acumen; <u>He knew how to make a shilling and how to hold on to it.</u>

I wonder if Dickens wasn't inspired by today's scripture, when he conceived his tale of Scrooge, when he wrote about the nocturnal visit of Scrooge's tortured partner, Jacob Marley, and then by three ghosts—Christmas Past, Christmas Present, and Christmas Future?

I think, knowing that Dickens was Christian, it is quite possible that Jesus' parable might have inspired the message for his tale, a story about being convinced about one thing and then being RE-convinced—being repentant.

We can find people in many places with strong convictions, sometimes very bad convictions:

A number of years ago we watched in horror as we saw on television the results of some people who were convinced that Jim Jones was a prophet who had the answers to life. More than 1100 people followed Jones to a poisonous death because they were convinced that he was right. Being convinced of something doesn't make it right.

Many people will not go near the water, or at least not in the deep end of a pool, because they are convinced that they would drown if they did.

Some people are convinced they should never spank their child.

Some people are convinced their money is only safe under the mattress.

There are others who are convinced that flying is not safe.

Some of our convictions may seriously limit what we will or will not do.

This morning I'd like us to look at 'being convinced', convinced that God raised Jesus from the dead.

The parable that Jesus told is a colorful story, a one act play in two scenes. Picture a great house on the hill. Its lawns and gardens slope gently away from the main house. There's a little stream that passes through the garden. Everything in the garden is beautifully manicured. Surrounding the entire yard is a high, wrought-iron fence, which comes together with two, large, gold, impressive-looking gates that are secured with the latest security system.

The house itself is large and spacious with many, many rooms. It has a two story portico in front.

Every lovely detail has been masterfully crafted. The owners of the house take great pride in their home.

A rich man lives there. He matches the house well. He has seen to every detail in his dress. He wears only the finest clothes. He drives a red Porsche and has the biggest yacht in the marina. The rich man enjoys the finest of everything. Even his food is gourmet. He sent his chef to a French cooking school for a year. The rich man knows how to enjoy his good life.

Outside his yard, though, is a very different picture. A man lies at the rich man's gate. This poor man has nothing except a name; his name is Lazarus. There is a great chasm of difference between the rich man and Lazarus. Lazarus is hungry and eaten up with sores—big, nasty ulcers on much of his body. Lazarus can only look up at the big house on the hill and imagine the food that is being left uneaten and wish that he could be one of the pups under the table, then he would be able to lick up a few morsels for himself.

But there is no passing through the gate into the yard and the house of the rich man. Lazarus must remain hungry and sick and cold and uncared for.

The picture of the two men and their worlds is strikingly different and sad in its unjustness. The picture seems to cry out for some act of fair dealing to come to it, for someone to tilt the scale in the direction of fairness for Lazarus.

But that is the end of Scene One; the curtain comes down.

Scene Two has some similarities to Scene One. There is again a great house with a wonderful lawn and garden surrounding it. This time, however, our man Lazarus is in the great dining hall, resting on a lounge chair, leaning on the bosom of another man, his great-great-great grandfather Abraham. Lazarus has been enjoying the finest in dining in the banquet hall. He's also enjoying the fellowship of his other kin in this heavenly hall.

Surrounding the garden in this scene, however, is not a high fence with an impossible gate, but a chasm too deep and treacherous for anyone to cross. It is a permanent barrier between the wonders of the heavenly mansion and what lies beyond.

But our eyes can take us beyond the chasm, even if a body could not cross it physically.

And in this outside place a grim, even terrifying scene—orange, leaping flames, heavy acidic smoke, heat scorching the air. Nobody could exist in such an arena, but then we catch sight of the rich man, who is apparently engulfed in the flames, yet not being consumed. We look in horror at the man. What an awful place is this!

The rich man has found himself in a new position suddenly. It seems he has died and his reward from his time on earth is not more beautiful gardens and sumptuous gowns and meals; it is eternal fires and thirst that will not be quenched.

Once the second act has opened and the scene is set, a conversation begins, unlike any I've heard before. The man who's been thrown into Hell is able to see beyond the inferno and across the chasm and even into the banquet hall where the former pathetic figure of Lazarus is enjoying the wonders of Heaven.

The man cries out to Abraham, "Father Abraham, have mercy on me and send Lazarus to dip the tip of his finger in water and cool my tongue, for I am in agony in these flames."

What's happening? The tables have turned: the last has become first, and the first now suffers in the last place in God's kingdom that anyone would want to be.

We know the end of the story. The rich man is not to be satisfied. He has made his bed, and now he must lie in it. So now, recognizing his fate, he asks Father Abraham to send Lazarus to his house, for he has five brothers who will be doomed to this terrible inferno if they are not warned.

But Abraham replies, "They have Moses and the Prophets, but they have not listened to them."

"But', cries the man, 'if someone comes to them from the dead, they will change their ways; they will repent."

And Abraham answers, "If they do not listen to Moses and the prophets, neither will they be convinced even if someone rises from the dead.'

Father Abraham wasn't so positive about people responding to God's word. Moses and the prophets had already come and spoken God's word to them. People had heard before. Presumably they knew the prophet's message: God delights not in showy gifts at the altar, but a sacrifice of the heart. Justice and righteousness are what God wants--for people to care for their fellow humans.

The former rich man had his opportunity. He had, no doubt, heard God's word spoken by the prophets, but he took no action. The former rich man had been blocked, if you will, by the high fence around his garden, which protected him from the outside world. It kept him from listening to the prophets and being convinced that he could do something to help. The high fence that stood between the rich man and Lazarus was more than just a physical structure; it was the abyss that eventually kept him from heaven.

Is that true for us today? What high gates or deep chasms block our hearing or listening to God's word? What structures are keeping us from being convicted of it? What wrought-iron gate will keep us from seeing the needs in this world that we can touch? What barrier might keep us out of heaven?

Jesus spoke of the troubles people face in hearing God's word when he told the parable of the Sower and the Seeds. He pointed to the three reasons people are not convinced of God's word. You could say that each of the three are barriers to being convinced of God's word

1—Not understanding: I've heard it said, and it is probably especially true of our Bible Belt here, that there are many people who have had just enough experience with the Christian faith to be inoculated from the real thing. That is, many people may have had some experience with church or faith in Christ, but they did not understand it. They never grew in their faith. They had nothing to support their faith when unbelievers pooh-poohed it. They backed away, afraid to oppose strong opinions of others. They never discovered the blessing of living in a personal relation with the risen Christ. They never learned to trust and obey. They don't have hope for their future, which is a promise to those who know and love Him.

2. Troubles and Cares: Some people hear the Word of God and are all excited about it to begin with, but then reality reminds them that there are serious cares and troubles in this world, and they turn their focus from Go to the troubles and get lost in their worry. It's certainly understandable for people to be aware of pain and grief and suffering, especially when it's right in front of us, but it's too bad that people would separate themselves and their troubles from the One who can help, the One who heals, the One who gives hope and future.

3—The lure of riches and excitement of the world. That's where so many people are today. The world has always had alluring places, but with the advent of the media, advertising, and fast transportation, it seems to be very available to everyone at the touch of a mouse, click of a remote, the zip of a Master Card. We can even be aware that the alluring things of this world are simply that—temporal pleasures that won't last, but that doesn't stop us from seeing them, thinking about them, and enjoying them. The things of this world, for the most part, are not really wrong, but the trouble comes when they take over our lives, pushing out the One who belongs in the first place—our God.

How do we hear God's word today? God's word comes through many different voices, but it always comes because of the inspiration of the Holy Spirit:

God's work can come

- From scripture

- From the radio

- From a letter from a friend

- From the morning song of a jay announcing the birth of a new day

- From the smell of a wonderful meal inviting us to come, eat, and celebrate life.

- From the words of a neighbor or fellow Christian, sharing a time when God acted in their lives

- From the memory of times gone by, maybe a youth group gathered around a campfire

- From a fictional story in a book that tells of Christian value

- From words we remember from our parents or grandparents when we were small

- From the bright eyes of children who shine the love of God up at us.

- From words that form in our hearts when we've told God how we failed, how we hurt others, how we could have done better, …And then the LORD responding, "I forgive you. Tomorrow you can get up and try again."

There are countless ways that God speaks to us. When we recognize that it is God who is speaking to us, how can we not be convinced to change our ways and to follow him?

Jesus is the Word of God. St. John calls him that in the prologue of his gospel—"in the beginning was the Word, and the word was with God and the Word was God. He was in the beginning with God. All things came into being through him, and without him not one thing came into being … and the Word became flesh and lived among us, and we beheld his glory, the glory as of a father's only son, full of grace and truth." (John 1:1-3;14)

Jesus is the final piece in this picture. Abraham told the rich man that even if someone rises from the dead, it will not convince some, for they will not listen to God's word.

Jesus rose from the dead. His rising is THE point of convincing. Remember Thomas? He said he would not be convinced until he placed his hand in Jesus' torn side himself. Then he would believe. But when the risen Christ appeared before Thomas, he was convinced, completely convinced. Nothing more was necessary. His life was then ordered after that one fact: That Jesus had risen from the dead.

- Therefore he would follow Jesus

- Therefore he would go to the ends of the earth for Jesus

- Therefore he would share his faith with anyone and everyone he met.

- Therefore he would die a martyr's death in far off India.

Dickens' story of Scrooge shows that he was more than impressed with his visitors that night. He was scared into repentance of his old, miserly ways, and he became a beacon of kindness and a marvelous example of charity and love to all. He was convinced!

Who can forget that final scene when Scrooge woke to discover that his visitors had not been real, that it was now Christmas morning, and he still had time to change the way he lived.

Scrooge was more than happy to share blessings with all that he met. He quickly sent the biggest goose in the market to the Cratchit family and then spent the day with this own kin, rejoicing in Christ's birth.

The good news is that God wants us to listen to his Word and be convinced. God never stops appealing to us through Jesus. Let us be convinced!

Luke 17:1-4

Jesus said to his disciples, *'Occasions for stumbling are bound to come, but woe to anyone by whom they come! It would be better for you if a millstone were hung around your neck and you were thrown into the sea than for you to cause one of these little ones to stumble. Be on your guard! If another disciple sins, you must rebuke the offender, and if there is repentance, you must forgive. And if the same person sins against you seven times a day, and turns back to you seven times and says, 'I repent,' you must forgive.'*

Not an Option

Have you ever heard how a monkey is caught in the jungle? It seems that a trap is set for the monkey. To make the trap, you must first hollow out a gourd, leaving an opening just large enough for the monkey to reach into the gourd. Place a sweet treat inside the gourd; then attach a vine to the gourd and stake the other end of the vine in the ground somewhere out of sight.

An unsuspecting monkey will smell the treat inside the gourd and reach inside to collect the sweet morsel. However, the opening, which is just large enough for the monkey's paw to pass through, is too small for the clinched fist to pass back through. The monkey cannot escape as long as he hangs onto the treat. It's a simple thing, then, for the poacher to take the monkey!

That's the picture I want us to remember this morning. When we clutch onto something and refuse to let it go, we may find ourselves in a very, spiritually dangerous place!

That's what's happening to us when we don't forgive someone who has done us wrong. When we are unforgiving, we, like the money with his hand stuck in the gourd, are not free of the thing we are grasping, and we are in a dangerous place for our souls.

Our scripture today is about forgiveness.

Jesus tells us, several times in the gospels, that we

are to forgive others.

In Matthew's gospel we hear Peter asking Jesus about forgiving others. Peter began by pointing to the Jewish law, which dictated if someone sins against you, you must forgive up to three times, but Peter, thinking that he was catching on to Jesus' new way of thinking, asked the LORD if disciples should need to forgive as many as seven times.

Jesus surprised Peter by saying, 'It is not seven times to forgive another, but seventy-seven times!" [You may remember this number to be seventy times seven, which is how the number was translated in the KJV.] Jesus' point is that it is a very big number of times we need to forgive.

Then Jesus told a parable to more clearly express what he meant:

The Kingdom of heaven can be compared to a king who was planning to settle his accounts with his slaves. There was one slave who owed the king a great deal of money, something like fifteen year's worth of wages. The slave was brought before the king who demanded the money. The slave could not repay the king. The king ordered that the slave be sold with his wife in payment. But the slave fell on his knees and begged, 'Have patience with me, and I will repay you everything.' The king, out of pity for the slave, released the man and completely forgave his debt.'

'But!' Jesus continued, 'that same slave went out from the king and came upon a fellow slave who owed him money—one hundred denarii, which would have been worth 100 day's wages. The man seized his fellow slave by the throat and demanded that he be paid in full right then. The fellow slave fell on his

knees and pleaded with the man, 'Have patience with me, and I will pay you.' But the first slave refused. He had the man thrown into prison until his debt was paid. When the fellow slaves saw what had transpired, they saw the injustice of what had just happened, so they went to the king and told him. The king summoned the slave and said, 'You wicked slave!'

I forgave you all that debt because you pleaded with me. Should you not have had mercy on your fellow slave, as I have had mercy on you? Then the king had the man handed over to be tortured until he would pay his debt.'

Jesus added, '*So my heavenly Father will also do to anyone of you, if you do not forgive your brother or sister from your heart.'*

That story seems to say that our being forgiven is tied to our forgiving others.

Can that be right?

Does the forgiveness that Jesus offers me hinge on my forgiving others?

Remember, when Jesus taught the disciples to pray he included, '*forgive us our trespasses as we forgive those who trespass against us.'*

Then, after teaching the prayer, Jesus added, '*For as you forgive others their trespasses, your heavenly Father will also forgive you; but if you do not forgive others, neither will your Father forgive your trespasses.'*

Jesus calls us to forgive those who have offended us, or hurt us, or betrayed us, or built up some debt to us. If we were not forgiven ourselves, we would not have had a mandate to be forgiving, but we HAVE been forgiven. The two forgivenesses are bound together. FORGIVENESS IS NOT AN OPTION!

Forgiving others seems to be one of those 'yeses' we say as Christians. That is to say, when we started following Jesus we said, ;'Yes, LORD, I will follow you; I will go where you tell me to go; I will do what you want me to do.' That initial 'yes' implies other, yet unknown 'yeses' that will come upon us down the road as we walk with Jesus. Those 'yeses' may not be easy; and those 'yeses' WILL include forgiving others.

Before we get into how to forgive, I think it would be helpful to think about what forgiveness is not. Dr. Robert D. Enright suggests five things that forgiveness is not:

Forgiveness is not forgetting: Our memories are too good to be able to forget things that were bad enough to need forgiveness. Deep hurt can rarely be wiped out of our awareness. Time can fade the pain of some abuse, but the memory of it won't be forgotten completely.

When we are called to forgive, we are not expected to completely forget the event.

Forgiving is not reconciling: Reconciling takes two parties, both the abuser and the offended must agree to be reconciled. When we forgive another we are not expecting or requiring the offending party to be reconciled. [I'm sure it would be good if both parties would agree, but that is not the dynamic of forgiveness.]

A good example is what Jesus did for us. He came

to reconcile us t the Father through his sacrifice. God is willing to reconcile with us, but we have to be willing to be reconciled, or it doesn't work. Both sides have to agree for reconciliation.

Forgiveness is not condoning: We are not asked to excuse someone's bad or hurtful behavior when we forgiven. The abuse still occurred, and we don't have to ignore it. We can forgive without excusing the person who hurt us.

Forgiveness is not dismissing: The evil deed still hurt and caused pain. It would be wrong to pretend it was inconsequential or insignificant. If we've been wronged, the offence should be taken seriously. The deed did take place.

Forgiveness is not pardoning: A pardon is a legal transaction that releases the offender from the consequences of an action such as a penalty. Forgiveness is a personal transaction that releases the one offended from the event. Let me reiterate: Forgiveness is a personal transaction that releases the one offended from the event.

Bishop Willimon once wrote: 'The human animal is not supposed to be good at forgiveness. Forgiveness is not some innate, natural, human emotion. Vengeance, retribution, violence, these are natural, human qualities. It is natural for the human animal to defend itself, to snarl, to bit back when bitten. Forgiveness is not natural. It is not a universal human virtue.

What does it mean to forgive?

The dictionary tells us forgiveness means

- To give up resentment or a claim to requital for

- To grant relief from payment of

- To cease to feel resentment against [the offender]

Forgiveness is very much part of the Christian life, and maybe it is a part of our lives every day.

I remember the time I gave my life to Jesus, many years ago. There was a period of about three weeks afterwards that I found various memories of mine that began popping up in my mind—things like anger over something, irritation at someone, grudges, all sorts of unsavory things. And I felt the nudging of the Holy Spirit to forgive the people who had hurt me, and to 'come clean', if you would. I was carrying around a lot of stuff that needed to be let go. So I spent those few weeks ridding myself of those old, unforgiven pains.

I believe it's very important that we do that to have a healthy, Christian life. We must not let painful stuff build up that need to be let go and forgiven.

Recently I learned something more, something you might call 'the rest of the story' about forgiveness.

This is not the first time I've preached about forgiveness. I spoke this sermon to my church in Huntsville a couple of years ago. I was using Matthew's gospel, which has Jesus and Peter in conversation and the parable about the wicked slave.

When I began working on today's sermon, I wanted to use a Lucan text, if possible, so I thought I'd see if

Luke had a similar passage to Matthew's.

And there is, but there are a couple of differences. The Lucan passage says that if a fellow disciple sins against you, you must rebuke him or her and if he or she repents, you must forgive. Even if this happens seven times in a day, you must forgive.

Rebuking and repenting were added to the formula about forgiving. In other words, if/when you have been harmed, you have the responsibility to the offender to inform him or her that something untoward has occurred and you have been hurt.

I hadn't really thought about that before, and I imagine that's a place where we Christians don't go. How often have we gone to someone who has hurt us and rebuked him or her?

There was a situation that occurred to me when we were in Huntsville. A woman I knew there hurt me, and when the event took place I knew I would need to forgive her. And I had tried to do just that, but the thought of her words had continued to plague me.

Then I read this verse, and I realized I needed to confront this woman and tell her how she had hurt me. So I wrote an email to her saying that [rebuking her], and then I hit he 'send' button.

The next day I got an amazing response from the woman! She admitted how badly she had acted and wrote a lengthy not telling me how she had been wrong and begged my forgiveness. She even included a prayer in her writing.

There was something about the email response that cleared the entire situation clean and finished. It's really done!

Learning to forgive is something that apples to every one of us here. There is not one person in this room who has not been hurt by someone at some time.

This scripture is a reminder to us to forgive our offenders, just as Christ has forgiven us.

There is a picture I'd like us to take away from this sermon. It is the picture of our hand—an opened hand, not one closed in a fist. When we have a problem with someone

- Some bad experience

- A blowout with a colleague

- Abuse

- Betrayal

- Whatever it is

And we keep hold on it, we are continuing to be harmed by the thing. We are not allowing God to heal us from the event, and we are carrying it with us into future relationships. [I can imagine that some of us have kept such events alive by telling others of those memories and in some way even enjoying the attention and the sympathy we get from the telling.]

Just remember your hand, gripping the thing and not letting go. You have then fallen into the trap, like the monkey who can't escape being caught, because his hand is stuck in the gourd. He's trapped. He's going to be somebody's dinner tonight.

Now imagine what we should be like, letting go of the things we're hanging on to—that we need to let go of. When I mentioned this subject earlier, I believe everyone here thought to him or herself about some situation, some person, with whom we're not too happy, whom we are still nursing a grudge or some kind of anger. You have no more reason to claim it, and you have no more interest in it. You have to let it go! What freedom is ours! That's forgiveness!

Luke 17: 1-10

17 ¹⁻³ᵃ Then Jesus said to his disciples, "It is inevitable that there should be pitfalls, but alas for the man who is responsible for them! It would be better for that man to have a millstone hung round his neck and be thrown into the sea, than that he should trip up one of these little ones. So be careful how you live.

³ᵇ⁻⁴ "If your brother offends you, take him to task about it, and if he is sorry, forgive him. Yes, if he wrongs you seven times in one day and turns to you and says, 'I am sorry' seven times, you must forgive him."

⁵ And the apostles said to the Lord, "Give us more faith."

⁶ And he replied, "If your faith were as big as a grain of mustard seed, you could say to this fig-tree, 'Pull yourself up by the roots and plant yourself in the sea', and it would do what you said!"

7-10 "If any of you has a servant ploughing or looking after the sheep, are you likely to say to him when he comes in from the

fields, 'Come straight in and sit down to your meal'? Aren't you more likely to say, 'Get my supper ready: change your coat, and wait until I eat and drink: and then, when I've finished, you can have your meal'? Do you feel particularly grateful to your servant for doing what you tell him? I don't think so. It is the same with yourselves—when you have done everything that you are told to do, you can say, 'We are not much good as servants, for we have only done what we ought to do.'"

<u>SPEAKING OF FAITH</u>

This morning we'll start out with a verse to learn: *"without faith it is impossible to please God, for whoever would approach him must believe that he exists and that he rewards those who seek him."* (Heb. 11:6) (repeat with cong. Several times: without faith it is impossible to please God.)

It seems that Luke pulled together four sayings of Jesus, which we read at the beginning of chapter Seventeen. These sayings were not all spoken one after the next by Jesus. In fact, you can read a couple of them in different situations in the Synoptic Gospels. The sayings are all about faith, so that is our topic today.

Faith is what brings us together as Christians.

The first saying begins, *"Occasions for stumbling are bound to come, but woe to anyone by whom they come! It would be better for you if a millstone were hung around your neck and you were thrown into the sea than for you to cause one of these little ones to stumble."*

If we say or do something that causes someone else to fall into temptation, hurt himself or to hurt others, we carry the blame. We know that in law if someone knows about a crime and does not try to impede the crime—by alerting the police—that person is an accomplice. An accomplice is just as guilty as the person who did the crime.

I met a woman in Stevenson several years ago who 'bought' a refrigerator that she knew was stolen. She was a young woman with three little children, but she spent several years in prison because she was an accomplice to the crime.

Jesus was talking about anyone who might cause another to stumble from their faith. How do you suppose that could happen? That's a sticky subject, because not everyone thinks the same way that we do. In fact, not everyone here thinks the same way.

We are here, gathered together, because we are people of faith, but we might not each express our faith the same way. When we all repeat The Apostle's Creed, then we are all sounding the same, but even then, it might be that we would interpret the words differently.

We might cause someone else to stumble if we are so adamant about our way of expressing faith that we bludgeon others with words to make them see it our way. The problem is that faith is sacred.

Faith is what we need to walk with the LORD each day, and if our faith is jeopardized, then we are suddenly set adrift with no mooring to hang on to. We could be suddenly set out to sea, so to speak, without a means to get back to shore.

If we damage someone's simple faith (what Jesus called 'a little one's' faith) we are responsible for them. I find myself treading very lightly when I run into someone who has faith that is not well understood, or whose faith is different from my own. Rather than engaging in some verbal fisticuffs about religion, I will probably steer more to the action side of the picture. I might ask: "How does your faith inform what you do in this world? How does your faith guide you to love God and your neighbor more?" I am convinced that if a person is serving God and neighbor they will NOT hate Jesus. Jesus did say, *'If someone is not against me, he is for me.'* Maybe that person can come to know Jesus through the back door—practicing faith until he has it.

There are some Christian communities who have practices that seem odd to me. For instance, there are communities who get into excessive laughing. They are falling all over the floor in great, heaving laughter. (It's supposed to show being full of the Holy Spirit.) I don't know if that does or does not prove their faith, but if they are not also showing love of God and neighbor, then their laughing means nothing.

There is something very sacred about faith, something that Jesus doesn't want us to damage. The dictionary says: "Faith is confidence, trust, reliance on God, because God is worthy of that trust." God is worthy because we have seen God being faithful before.

If we fail, our faith has been broken; for a moment or maybe forever, we no longer are following after the One who gives us hope. Instead, we have allowed the 'ME inside' to take over. Rather than relying on God, and imitating God's goodness, we fail and try to navigate dangerous waters of this world on our own.

Jesus knew there are many things that can cause a person to stumble, to lose faith, but his warning to us, is DON'T BE THE ONE WHO CAUSES SOME ONE TO FALL.

The second saying is, " *[3]Be on your guard! If*

another disciple sins, you must rebuke the offender, and if there is repentance, you must forgive. ⁴And if the same person sins against you seven times a day, and turns back to you seven times and says, 'I repent,' you must forgive."

Forgiveness is part of faith. At one time or another we all fail. We manage to hurt ourselves and we manage to hurt others. We need forgiveness. We find we must ask forgiveness. It's a big step for us to ask forgiveness, because it means we have humbled ourselves to God and to another, recognizing how we have caused pain and that we were wrong in doing so. We ask forgiveness of the other.

On the other side of that transaction we, who have been hurt, are called to forgive the other. That's another big step for us. We may have been badly abused; we may have lost something important; we may have been terribly embarrassed. There's untold ways we could have been hurt, but Jesus says if someone asks for forgiveness we must forgive. Even if there are multiple examples of the same crime!

Even in the same day! Forgiving others is not an option, if they ask for it.

Jesus told the disciples to be ready to forgive again and again. He didn't seem to leave any wiggle room, either. He didn't say, "If you feel like it, go ahead and forgive." He didn't say, "Forgive once, twice, but not more than three times." He said forgive seven times in a day, and I take that to mean often. In fact, who's counting?

Forgiving is part of faith. Because God has forgiven us, we forgive others. It's not a matter of weighing out how much this pain or that mistake was worth and forgiving just that much. It's about being obedient and being like God. We all affirm 'forgive us our trespasses as we forgive those who trespass against us.'

Maybe the disciples thought that was a tall order— to keep on forgiving. So they asked, "Lord, increase our faith." Do you suppose they thought such a requirement would need more faith? The Lord replied, *"If you had faith the size of a mustard seed, you could say to this mulberry tree, 'Be uprooted and planted in the sea,' and it would obey you."*

Apparently faith is able to do a lot more than we know. *Remember 'with God all things are possible.'* (Matt 19:26) The important thing is to have faith, faith in the one who is worthy of our confidence, trust and reliance.

I'm not sure what exactly builds up faith, but there are two parts of faith: head and heart. We may have a lot of information about God and Jesus and the church, but that is only head knowledge and not enough to carry us to the end. Information is very useful and helpful. My time at Wesley seminary working on my Master's of Divinity was very good for securing my faith. It helped me to understand so much of the big picture of faith and how God is working in Christ to save this world. But information alone is only half the equation. The second half is our heart. It is recognizing that Jesus is a real person who is deeply interested in being our friend, who has gone to extremes to care and save us, who fills us with his Spirit. The two, head and heart, work together to carry us along our path as we follow Christ.

The disciples asked Jesus to increase their faith. Jesus is faithful to give us what we ask for when we ask for what he wants to give us. He told us that he is very willing to give us the Holy Spirit every time we ask.

That was the third saying, but the strangest one came last: *⁷"Who among you would say to your slave who has just come in from plowing or tending sheep in the field, 'Come here at once and take your place at the table'? ⁸Would you not rather say to him, 'Prepare supper for me, put on your apron and serve me while I eat and drink; later you may eat and drink'? ⁹Do you thank the slave for doing what was commanded? ¹⁰So you also, when you have done all that you were ordered to do, say, 'We are worthless slaves; we have done only what we ought to have done!'"*

That all sounds pretty hard hearted, even for a slave owner. Maybe I'm just naïve.

We've never lived in a world where there was slavery, so I don't, know. Maybe that's how slaves were treated after a hard day's work picking cotton, then they came into the plantation house and waited on their masters over dinner. (I must have thought that there were some slaves who did domestic work, and it would be them who prepared the meals and served the owners and those coming in from the long day's work in the sun.)

Jesus, of course, was referring to slavery as it

was in his day. Maybe slaves never had a moment of free time to do their own thing.

But what do slaves have to do with faith in the first place? I wondered. Maybe these four thoughts really don't hang together. This last picture—the slave working hard and log all day and then being expected to serve the master all evening long—how does it have anything to do with faith? Jesus said the slave works all day in the fields, comes into the house and prepares the meal and serves his master, and the only thanks he gets is a 'what did you expect?' from the master. "After all, you're my slave. You do for me what I want when I want it."

That really didn't fit with the sayings about faith, and then I saw it. Jesus was not talking about people who were slaves. Jesus was talking about faith as a slave.

Jesus used the picture of a slave, someone who works hard for his master all day long, doing whatever the master requires. But he meant that faith is a servant to us.

Today we are servants of Christ, and our faith in Jesus is what allows us to serve him. "Faith is confidence, trust, reliance on God, because God is worthy of that trust." Faith is confidence, trust, reliance on Jesus because Jesus is worthy of that trust.

Remember what Paul wrote in Philippians, what is called the Kenosis? It was probably sung among the early Christians about Jesus.

5Let the same mind be in you that was in

Christ Jesus, 6who, though he was in the form of God, did not regard equality with God as something to be exploited, 7but emptied himself, taking the form of a slave, being born in human likeness. And being found in human form, 8*he humbled himself* and became *obedient to the point of death— even death on a cross.*

Jesus showed us how to be a servant, by his complete obedience to his Father. His faith in God was perfect; he believed in his calling and his purpose and his mission. His faith never waivered. Even in the garden when he was realizing the moment had arrived for his final sacrifice and the pain and torture he would be facing, he spoke those words we have come to cherish, *"Not my will but thine be done."*

Jesus' little saying about the slave who worked all day and was still required to serve his master in the evening hours is all about faith. We need our faith in the day time of our lives, our waking hours, the busy times, the times when much can be accomplished and the time when there are many temptations.

Our faith is not finished with its work at the end of the day—or at the end of our days—when we might like to take it easy, have some refreshment, put our feet up and close our eyes to the world. No, our faith is just as much required in those waning years as at any other time.

Jesus finished this last saying with *"So you also, when you have done all that you were ordered to do, say, "We are worthless slaves;*

we have done only what we ought to have done!"

That a humble attitude that we need. Let the host of the party come to us and move us to a position of honor if he desires. Our attitude must be humble before the LORD.

Remember the words of Psalm 116:15, *"Precious in the sight of the LORD is the death of his faithful ones."*

Our faith is our servant even to the last moment of our lives. That's what we must expect from our faith. We need it to carry us to our last breath on earth. Its' job is not over before that moment.

It occurs to me that we have another picture of that faithfulness. The picture is our hearts. Doesn't our faith reside in our hearts? That's often how it is spoken of in verse and scripture. Jeremiah wrote that God would write a new law on our hearts. (33) Our heart is a servant of our bodies; its work is not done until our last breath. And so our faith, which lives in our hearts, is not finished its work until that final moment when God calls us home.

Amen.

Luke 19: 1-10

19 *¹⁻⁵ Then he went into Jericho and was making his way through it. And here we find a wealthy man called Zacchaeus, a chief collector of taxes, wanting to see what sort of person Jesus was. But the crowd prevented him from doing so, for he was very short. So he ran ahead and climbed up into a sycamore tree to get a view of Jesus as he was heading that way. When Jesus reached the spot, he looked up and saw the man and said, "Zacchaeus, hurry up and come down. I must be your guest today."*

⁶⁻⁷ So Zacchaeus hurriedly climbed down and gladly welcomed him. But the bystanders muttered their disapproval, saying, "Now he has gone to stay with a real sinner."

⁸ But Zacchaeus himself stopped and said to the Lord, "Look, sir, I will give half my property to the poor. And if I have swindled anybody out of anything I will pay him back four times as much,"

⁹ Jesus said to him, "Salvation has come to this house today! Zacchaeus is a descendant of Abraham, and it was the lost the Son of Man came to seek— and to save."

SAINT ZAC

Jesus didn't travel alone. When Jesus went from town to town he moved with a group. We think of the group that went with Jesus as the Twelve Disciples. We think of them walking together along the pathways to the various towns. In my mind I see them moving as a group, never apart. But there were other times when there were more than the Twelve.

In fact there may have been a large crowd that followed Jesus from place to place.

Jesus was the big event in Palestine. Everyone talked about him. His fame was everywhere. Jesus' fame spread throughout the land. Even in the time when there was no media—no phones, no T.V., no internet, no documentaries, no telegraph or anything besides 'tell-a-woman', Jesus' fame spread quickly.

Of course it would. Jesus' was remarkable, and no one who met him could think otherwise. Even those people who feared Jesus' popularity recognized his fame; they also recognized the many miracles Jesus did.

Jesus knew he was on his final journey. He and his disciples had been traveling to Jerusalem. They made many stops along the way. They weren't in a hurry. They planned to celebrate the Passover in Jerusalem in the spring, but it wasn't yet time.

Today's story starts with the crowd. Jesus was coming to Jericho. As Jesus and his crowd made their way to the city the word spread that the traveling rabbi had come to Jericho! They quickly gathered around Jesus and began walking with him through the city streets.

Zacchaeus heard, too. He was excited just like everyone else. He wanted to see Jesus. But as much as he wanted to see Jesus, he had a problem. In fact, he had two problems. You see Zacchaeus was not a man of much full stature. He wasn't like King Saul who stood head and shoulders above all the rest of the men. Zacchaeus was more like a ten-year-old boy. He never attained a man's full height.

Zacchaeus made up for his less than full stature in other ways. His height might be less than average, but his mind was not. Zacchaeus was sharp. His wit was sharp. He knew how to figure, and he had been able to gather quite a nice estate from his cleverness.

But the other reason Zacchaeus feared he might not see Jesus was because no one liked him. In fact he was hated in his community.

It was pretty terrible. He couldn't join the men folk to sit and pass the time; he was not welcome in their presence. If he came up to the men in the town, they would get up and move away.

Zacchaeus was a tax collector. He didn't enjoy friendships among the people of his town. Everyone treated him as if he was a thief. Zacchaeus had a job working for the Romans, the hated oppressors of Judea. It was his job to collect the prescribed indirect taxes, tolls, tariffs, and customs fees in his area. It didn't bother the Romans if tax collectors added a little extra for themselves along the way. After all, they had to eat, too, so it was expected that their salary would come from the assessments they made the people. But tax collectors were known for their greed. They stole from their neighbors, and it was sanctioned by the Roman rulers.

As I was saying, Zacchaeus wanted to see Jesus.

Of course, Zacchaeus had been in crowds before and he knew he was seriously not able to see because of the crowds. Taller people would block his vision. How to fix the problem? What could he do?

Well, he quickly decided that he could climb that old sycamore tree in town. If he got up there before Jesus arrived, he could see the whole thing with a bird's eye view. He'd have the best seat in the house.

And that's what he did. Zacchaeus put all his dignity aside and ran as fast as he could move to the sycamore tree and began climbing. Its low limbs invited him into the tree. Once there he waited. It wasn't long before he began to see the crowd of people coming toward him. He could see the town's people, and then there were others that Zac didn't recognize. 'They must be Jesus' friends', he thought. 'They must be his traveling buddies.'

Suddenly the crowd stopped moving, in fact they stopped right at the tree where Zacchaeus was sitting overhead. Then Jesus looked up into the tree. He looked up and looked straight at Zacchaeus and spoke to him. Jesus said,

"Zacchaeus, hurry and come down; for I must stay at your house today".

"Zacchaeus! Hurry and come down; for I must stay at your house today."

That sounds like an invitation, although usually the one who does the inviting in the one who has the place for the invitee to come. Jesus was inviting Zacchaeus to more than dinner. Jesus was inviting Zacchaeus to be part of the Kingdom of God? He told them to leave their nets and boats and to come, follow him?

Isn't that what happened to Saul of Tarsus on the Road to Damascus? Saul was on his way to bring trouble to the Followers of the Way in Damascus when he was blinded by a great light, thrown to the ground, and Jesus spoke to him, *"Saul, Saul why are you persecuting me?* And Saul was told to go into Damascus and he would be told what to do.

All those were examples of Jesus calling people to follow him.

That was Zacchaeus' story, too. Jesus was calling him to put down his wrong way of life, to get to know Jesus and become part of Jesus' people: to follow Jesus.

Luke tells us that Zacchaeus made some promises when Jesus and Zacchaeus were together. They enjoyed one another's company over a nice meal first. Then Zacchaeus said, *'Look, half of my possessions, Lord, I will give to the poor; and I if I have defrauded anyone of anything I will pay back four times as much.***"**

Now there's repentance! Zac turned from his wrong doings and promised to set right whatever had been amiss before. He even followed the ancient formula of returning four-fold to anyone he had defrauded.

Those are the first steps in following Jesus.

We hear Jesus call us, we turn to Jesus, and we repent.

I don't suppose I've every heard Zacchaeus' name included with the Saints of the church, but surely he is a saint.

He must have continued on following Jesus after their meal together. That evening, that meeting with Jesus, changed Zac's life. He was no longer the hated chief tax collector; he was a follower of Jesus. He became an example for his neighbors to see how to follow the LORD.

*27-33 Then up came some of the Sadducees
(who deny that there is any resurrection)
and they asked him, "Master, Moses told
us in the scripture, 'If a man's brother
should die without any children, he
should marry the widow and raise up a
family for his brother.' Now, there were
once seven brothers. The first got married
and died childless, and the second and the
third married the woman, and in fact all
the seven married her and died without
leaving any children. Lastly, the woman
herself died. Now in the 'resurrection'
whose wife is she of these seven men, for
she belonged to all of them?"*

*34-38 "People in this world," Jesus replied,
"marry and are given in marriage. But
those who are considered worthy of
reaching that world, which means rising
from the dead, neither marry nor are
they given in marriage. They cannot die
any more but live like the angels; for
being children of the resurrection, they
are the sons of God. But that the dead are
raised, even Moses showed to be true in
the story of the bush, when he calls the
Lord 'the God of Abraham, the God of
Isaac, and the God of Jacob'. For God is
not God of the dead, but of the living. For
all men are alive to him."*

RESURRECTION ROAD

Today we are celebrating All Saint's Day. We want to remember saints we have known in our lives, who have passed before us. We should also learn of those whom we didn't know personally, who lived a life of faith in Christ in various ways and have helped to pass on faith in Christ to a new generation.

We've grown up with hearing the names of some of the saints. Some we know very well—St. Mary, St. Matthew, St. Mark, St. Luke, St. John, St Peter, St. Paul, and St. Francis, to name just a few.

Saints are people who have traveled the road of faith their whole lives, from the moment they came to faith in Christ.

Do you wonder how it is that the saints were able to keep on keeping on? How were they able to stay faithful to Christ always? Was there anything specific that they had to help them?

First, I would like to read a poem for you, one that I'll bet some of you know by heart. Some of you will remember with relish. The poem is by Robert Frost.

[The Road Not Taken by Robert Frost would be read here.]

Frost told in delightful poetry how he had encountered a fork in his path, and he chose to take the one less traveled by. And that choice made all the difference in his life.

The two different ways of thinking are about how we view life after death—whether there is such a thing as life after death or not. Is there such a thing as resurrection?

In Jesus' day there were two different groups of Jews who disagreed about the resurrection. One group did not believe in resurrection; the other group did.

Jesus had come to Jerusalem; He and his followers had just arrived there. He had brought the disciples to Jerusalem for the high, holy Festival of Passover. Jesus knew he would die that week. Jesus was acutely aware that this was his last week on earth. That knowledge had to permeate everything that Jesus did and said that week.

Sadducees were men of wealth and influence among the Jews. A group of them came to Jesus and posed a question to him. They thought this question would trip up Jesus. It seems that Sadducees and Pharisees were at odds about life after death.

Pharisees believed in resurrection; Sadducees did not. Sadducees believed that all there is to life is what you get on earth. Living in the present is all-important for them. It was the only way of life. Their best hope for future life would be living through their children.

The Sadducees realized that Jesus had come to Jerusalem, so they asked him a question, hoping to trip him up in his answer.

Listen to the question: *"Teacher, Moses wrote for us that if a man's brother dies, leaving a wife but no children, the man shall marry the widow and raise* up children for his brother. Now there were seven brothers; the first married and died childless; then the second and the third married her, and so in the same way all seven died childless. Finally, the woman also died. In the resurrection, therefore, whose wife will the woman be? For the seven had married her."

Jesus' answer surprised everyone who heard. He began by explaining that it is only in this age that people marry or are given in marriage. But he added, *"those who are considered worthy of a place in that age and in the resurrection from the dead neither marry or are given in marriage. And Jesus said, once people had obtained a resurrected life there is no death; they would be like the angels because they are children of the resurrection."*

There is no need for marriage in heaven, because children are not conceived or born in heaven; children come from this age and are then gathered into heaven later.

Jesus went on to point out that Moses himself had mentioned the resurrection when he wrote about Moses' encounter with the burning bush.

The LORD told Moses on that mountain that He was the God of Abraham, the God of Isaac, and the God of Jacob. In other words, those men were living with God. They were not dead, but living. Jesus said, *"God is not a God of the dead but God of the living, for to him all of them are alive."*

St. Luke tells us that the Sadducees were very impressed with Jesus' answer, and they told him so. Jesus had used their Scripture to prove to them that there is a resurrection.

Jesus proved that there was a resurrection-- already some of their ancestors were living life after death. He also mentioned that there was some sort of requirement to gain life after death.

Jesus said, *"those who are considered worthy of a place in that age and in the resurrection from the dead neither marry nor are given in marriage. "*

When I was reading that line I stopped short! I hadn't noticed those words before: "those who are considered worthy." St. Luke is the only gospel writer to include those words in this scene. He must have thought it important to remind his community that resurrection was not a given, that there is a requirement—being found worthy!

That leads me quickly to the question, "How might we be found worthy?"

Who decides if we're worthy?
Whose standard is being used?

Do you suppose we judge ourselves? When we get to the judgment seat, maybe we will be asked how we thought we did in this life.

I remember watching the Covenant Players in a play that was something like that.

The play begins in a small office furnished with a desk and two chairs. An angel sits in the chair behind the desk. Another angel leads the newly arrived candidate into the little office and points to the chair for the man to sit in. The angel behind the desk then looks over a long, long list of names, finds and entry, and proceeds to interrogate the candidate, asking him why he thinks he should expect to attain heaven. The nervous man hems and haws and says things like:

I believe in the Bible—the WHOLE Bible.

I was a member in good standing of my United Methodist Church.

I taught Sunday school to seventh graders for years.

I gave my pledge to the church.

I was active in the PTA and the Kiwanis Club. I loved my family.

I tried hard…..

The candidate is not sure what more to say. The angel doesn't seem to be impressed by any of the litany of good deeds that the person reels off.

Maybe our neighbors can help us out. Maybe after we are gone enough folks will say that we were good, or kind, or thoughtful, and that would satisfy requirements. We've known good people, one's that have led good lives; ones that have contributed to our community and raised beautiful children. They've been active in their churches and been productive in society. What if our friends sent a petition heavenward, stating how much they thought of us?

Would that give cause to open heaven's doors for us?

BUT GOD IS JUDGE! Jesus also told us that.

God is the one who makes the decisions. God is the one who counts a person worthy of resurrection.

Suddenly this discussion has become serious. There's nothing we can do to sway the judge. There's nothing we can do to inherit eternal life from our human position. Self-righteousness doesn't work. If we depend on our own merit not one of us will qualify.

But fortunately, God loves us … VERY MUCH!

And God wants us to live with Him. God provided a way to eternal life through His son Jesus. Jesus is righteous; He is completely worthy. He came from heaven to live on earth just because of his love for us. By his life, suffering and death, he did something that no one else could do. He provided a way for us to join him in everlasting life through belief in Him.

Jesus is the only righteous one. He is perfectly worthy. Our connection to Jesus is the Road to Resurrection. It is not through our own worthiness that we can attain heaven, but through our relationship with Christ that we are counted worthy.

When we come to faith in Christ we are counted as Righteous because of Christ's love for us.

I knew a woman when I was a country pastor. I was visiting her one day when she showed me all the jars of preserves she had just finished making. She showed me how she cooked the fruit down and made jam, poured it into the jars and then sealed them tight with wax. Once they had been sealed they would keep for a nice long time. Her family would enjoy the jam all winter.

Annie told me that she had been 'saved' many years earlier, when she was a teen. She had been baptized then. Annie told me that she had been 'sealed' by the Holy Spirit at that time. In other words, she was all set for heaven whenever that came along. She didn't have to worry about what she might do on earth, because she was already 'sealed' for eternity.

Annie explained that the sealing of the jam jars was a great picture for her to use for herself being 'sealed' for heaven. She figured her salvation was settled back in her youth; it didn't matter what she did now.

I worry about people that think that way. That's terribly short-sighted. The Resurrection Road, living in relationship with Jesus, and walking daily with him is not that simple.

Being counted worthy is a journey, not a one-time event. St. Paul wrote that he hopes to attain the resurrection, but he added, *"Not that I have already obtained this or have already reached the goal; but I press on to make it my own, because Christ Jesus has made me his own."* (Phil. 3:12)

We are counted worthy because we have a trust in Jesus, have a relationship with Jesus. Maybe we began hearing about Jesus when we were small, learning that Jesus is our friend. Later we heard that Jesus is the one who heals us and saves us. And we see the mess we make of our lives and reach out to Jesus to heal our souls.

We believe in Jesus to be our savior, our friend, our LORD. It's rather like a heavenly hand has reached from Heaven and touched us on the shoulder. Because of that connection with the LORD, we are considered worthy.

When we have that connection, we have not just this lifetime to live, we have eternity to live. And as we realize it, we begin to see things differently that we did before.

Jesus told the Sadducees that there was a resurrection. It was for those who were considered worthy of the new age, the heavenly age. And Jesus said those who inherit this life will live forever—like angels. There will be no death.

What is it about resurrection that is important anyway? What is the difference between a life lived believing in the resurrection and one that is lived without it?

When we have HOPE of the resurrection that means we won't despair. Even when really bad things happen to us, we believe that God is still in control that God's plans will overcome any obstacles.

In 1980 Dave and I were blessed with our third child, a beautiful little girl we named Kathryn Marie.

We called her Katie. Katie was a surprise to us; she arrived just before our son David's seventh birthday. We were thrilled to have Katie come into our lives.

Our two older kids, Leslie and David, were such wonders; we felt especially blessed to have yet one more child in our home. Katie was a beautiful little girl and a great joy to us.

It turns out that Katie was a bigger surprise than we'd even expected, because she died just a month later from something called Sudden Infant Death Syndrome--Crib Death. That will be 26 years ago this week. She was four weeks old; we were stunned when we realized that this new little one that God had been so gracious to give us, was no longer here. She had died in her sleep just as the snow was beginning to fall.

On that cold Tuesday morning Katie didn't wake up. No one knows what causes Crib Death, but for us it meant that she was no more. She was gone. No more pictures could be taken.

When the alarm clock sounded at six that morning, I asked Dave to go bring Katie to me from her little bedroom across the hall from ours. When he picked her up, Dave realized something was very wrong. He carried her to the bedroom door. He looked at me and said, "I think Katie is dead!" Then he placed her body back in the crib and came back to our room.

That was some moment. We didn't quite know what to do. We sat on the edge of the bed, holding one another's hands, and then we turned to the LORD in prayer. It was a simple prayer--something about being thankful that God was there with us, that we knew He loved Katie, and we knew that He was taking care of her now; we thanked Him for that. We also asked the LORD for guidance, because it seemed like the world had just stopped. Suddenly, nothing was the same. We asked the LORD for guidance for the road we needed to follow then.

That prayer didn't stop the pain or grief or shock

that flooded in on us. We experienced grief just like anyone else, but somehow, we believe that the healing process began for us that day. We didn't realize we were thinking theologically about the resurrection just then, but we did have hope for life after death. Katie was no longer with us; her body had no life in it. She had gone somewhere. We knew she had to be with our LORD, which is the best place to be.

We can choose which road we will follow on our journey through life. If we choose the road of unbelief, we have no reason to hope. We will have to stumble through life on our own strength and there won't be a life after death for us. When we choose the Resurrection Road, the road of belief in Jesus, we have so much more. We have hope for today and tomorrow. We have a wonderful friend who will accompany us each day on our journey, and there will be life everlasting in God's kingdom.

Two roads diverge in our lives today. Let us take the Resurrection Road for that will make all the difference.

Luke 24: 13-35

13-17 Then on the same day we find two of them going off to Emmaus, a village about seven miles from Jerusalem. As they went they were deep in conversation about everything that had happened. While they were absorbed in their serious talk and discussion, Jesus himself approached and walked along with them, but something prevented them from recognizing him. Then he spoke to them, "What is all this discussion that you are having on your walk?"

18 They stopped, their faces drawn with misery, and the one called Cleopas replied, "You must be the only stranger in Jerusalem who hasn't heard all the things that have happened there recently!"

19-21a "What things?" asked Jesus. "Oh, all about Jesus, from Nazareth. There was a man—a prophet strong in what he did and what he said, in God's eyes as well as the people's. Haven't you heard how our chief priests and rulers handed him over for execution, and had him crucified? But we were hoping he was the one who was to come and set Israel free ...

21b-24 "Yes, and as if that were not enough, it's getting on for three days since all this happened; and some of our womenfolk have disturbed us profoundly. For they went to the tomb at dawn, and then when they couldn't find his body they said that they had a vision of angels who said that he was alive. Some of our people went straight off to the tomb and found things just as the women had described them—but they didn't see him!"

25-26 Then he spoke to them, "Aren't you failing to understand, and slow to believe in all that the prophets have said? Was it not inevitable that Christ should suffer like that and so find his glory?"

27-29 Then, beginning with Moses and all the prophets, he explained to them everything in the scriptures that referred to himself. They were by now approaching the village to which they were going. He gave the impression that he meant to go on further, but they stopped him with the words, "Do stay with us. It is nearly evening and soon the day will be over."

30-32 So he went indoors to stay with them. Then it happened! While he was sitting at table with them he took the loaf, gave thanks, broke it and passed it to them. Their eyes opened wide and they knew him! But he vanished from their sight. Then they said to each other, "Weren't our hearts glowing while he was with us on the road, and when he made the scriptures so plain to us?"

33-34 And they got to their feet without delay and turned back to Jerusalem. There they found the eleven and their friends all together, full of the news— "The Lord is really risen—he has appeared to Simon now!"

35 Then they told the story of their walk, and how they recognized him when he broke the loaf.

<u>IT'S HIM!</u>

Such a day! Such terrible happenings! Indeed, the men had been consumed with the news for days. There was nothing else they could think about. There was only one subject and everyone was focused on it. How quickly the news had spread. If someone had not initially known, by witnessing things as they unfolded, then surely they knew by that evening. The news was that big, that thunderous, that consuming. It was the one thing that everyone was talking about.

The news was tragic, more than tragic; it was the most awful in so many ways at once.

The news was about loss, loss of a good friend, a dear man, an amazing teacher, a miracle worker, a man of compassion, of truth, of love, of goodness. There was no one you could even compare Jesus to, because he was so far above and beyond other leaders. His words were so wonderful. When he spoke, all around him stopped and listened as if his words held the meaning of life itself. Then everything changed! It changed and can never be changed back. Jesus had been killed! He had been sentenced to die, scourged within an inch of his life and then hung on a cross to die. It was so awful, Words could not tell of the horror of the whole thing. Yet words were all they had. What else could speak of the pain they now felt?

Then he appeared--a stranger on the road. He caught up with them and fell into step with them as they made their way to Emmaus. "So", said the stranger, "what were you two talking about in such deep tones? Is something amiss?"

How can you ask? They wondered. "Are you the only man in this whole country who does not know the news?"

And on they talked. They told the man of the terrible events of the week gone by and how much they hurt now.

That day has overtones of some of the events we've just been through. With the Trade Center attacks, we were consumed with the news for days. Everyone asked, "Where were you when it happened? Did you see it as it occurred?" There was nothing else we could think about. There was only one subject on everyone's lips, and on all the media. The news had spread. If someone had not initially known, by witnessing things as they unfolded, they knew by that evening. The news was that big, that thunderous, that consuming. It was the topic that was on everyone's lips.

We knew, even as the stories unfolded, that our lives would not be the same ever again, at least as far as feeling safe and protected here in our own country is concerned. We are still reeling from the events of September 11th. It will continue to be in our memory for the rest of our lives.

The two situations sound much the same. The world of the disciples had been so shattered, yet something very wonderful came into their lives and turned them around.

The stranger listened carefully to all the men had to say, and then he spoke. He seemed to take the conversation a whole new direction. The next thing you knew, he was talking about the prophets and what they had foretold about a servant who had to suffer. Did they not remember those writings in Isaiah?

Somehow as the stranger spoke, their pain had lifted and they became engrossed in his words. The stranger was more than interesting to listen to; he held their attention completely, and opened up Scripture for them in a way they had not experience before, except.....

By then they had arrived at the inn where they had planned to stay the night, at an inn in the town of Emmaus. But they didn't want to see the stranger leave, so they asked him to continue with them as they stopped for the evening meal.

The stranger agreed. He would sup with them.

Somehow the pain, which had been with the two for the past three days had left. They were really enjoying this stranger, who had such interest in them.

Then the hostess brought a loaf of bread, fresh from the oven, over to them. There's nothing more wonderful than fresh bread right straight from the oven. She placed it in front of the stranger, and he picked up the loaf, raised it to heaven, gave thanks to God for it. Then he broke the bread ...

The two travelers stared at the man. They sat, glued to their seats, watching every move of the man that sat with them. As he broke the bread and the wonderful smell of the fresh bread wafted out across the table, they knew!

They knew the truth. They knew who the stranger was. It was as if they had had scales on their eyes before, because now they knew! They realized that the stranger was no stranger at all, but he was their LORD, their friend, and their master, ... alive!

Of course, it was Jesus. Jesus came back into their lives and showed himself alive! He had risen from the dead and came back to be with them.

Christ' resurrection, the day he came back from the grave, is the event has changed the rest of the events in this world.

Think of it. When the terrorists attacked our country, hitting wicked blows to two of the greatest markers in our country, we were shocked, hurt, and incredulous, but something else has happened, too.

We've seen an outpouring of goodness from all sorts of unexpected places since the moment the first attack became known.

People have been going out of their way, sometimes even traveling long distances to help in our crisis. The blood banks are filled and continue to be filled. They now say there is more than enough food, water and supplies for the immediate disaster in New York.

Prayers are being said in new places. People are going out of their way to be nice to one another.

Red, white and blue colors abound everywhere, as people are showing their patriotism and their faith in God's goodness.

How come this is happening? I think we could have expected some help, but we are seeing an outpouring of caring and encouraging and reaching out in a hundred ways to those who were hurt or needy from Sept 11th.

We can feel the outpouring of compassion and caring from folks all around our nation. We can feel it because it is very real, and it is shows us that God's Spirit is with us in this time.

Do you recognize that when good things happen, God's Spirit is there working, being present in the goodness?

I have been pleased to see some of the responses that our government is taking as we work to untangle and pursue a way to bring to justice the evil doers, and yet not attack helpless families, particularly women and children of third world countries. I watched tons and tons of food being unloaded off planes, which is destined for the people of Afghanistan.

When the travelers who were on their way to Emmaus thought back on their afternoon and the stranger that had joined them on the road, they realized that something very special had happened. While they were in the stranger's company, somehow they were no longer caught in the grip of the deep sorrow and grief that had held them tightly before.

Although they didn't recognize the stranger right then, there was something about him that caused them to lay aside the pain they had been their constant companion and to listen to him.

Afterwards they thought about that afternoon and realized that something had been happening while they walked along. Something familiar, yet at the same time different, was growing inside them. After the initial exchange of words, they had been quickly drawn to the stranger. They had hung on every word that he spoke, as if what he said was somehow very important, that they should be sure to remember what he was saying about the prophets and their foretelling of a suffering servant who was to come.

They realized that the man who had joined their company had taken away their feeling of grief and had somehow comforted them by his presence. That was why they had sought to tarry with them and join them for supper at the inn.

Then! How had they missed it all before? When the stranger lifted the loaf toward heaven, gave thanks to God for his goodness and for providing this meal and had slowly broken the loaf before them.

They suddenly knew him. They knew his identity. He was their LORD! He had returned from the grave. He had come back to them! He had taken away their grief and given them comfort!

He had risen from the dead! They had recognized Jesus in the breaking of the bread!

The travelers had found him as he broke
the loaf before them. They knew he was
with them once again.

Jesus promised his disciples that he would be with
them to the end of time. He would not leave us or
forsake us ever. His promise is still good today.

God never changes.

Our faith in Christ tells us that when there is
serious trouble, when things go wrong, dangerous
times, painful events, scary business, we can count
on God's intervention. It is our job, as Christians, to
look for those events and to point them out to the
world, to help the world see God's work today.

Can we, like the disciples, see Jesus alive and
active in our world today? In these new times we
do see him. We see him in many ways.

Jesus himself gave us one wonderful way to
experience his presence, through the Holy Meal that
he instituted on the eve before his death. That meal,
the bread and the wine are wonderful symbols of
Jesus, yet they are more than that.

Some folks would want to say that the Lord's
Supper is only a time for us to remember the life
and death of Jesus, remember the great sacrifice
that he made for us and the significance of his
sacrifice— providing salvation and new life for us,
giving us keys to his Eternal Kingdom. Therefore,
the Lord's Supper is the time of personal inspection
of our lives and rethinking of our commitment to our
LORD and SAVIOR. The accent is on the believer,
how the believer thinks and commits and acts

That's all well and good. I have not the least objection to such thinking; In fact, I applaud it. We need to be committed to our LORD. He asks for our commitment. Our life in Christ is all about growing in his love and understanding. Commitment is an important piece to our Lord's Supper.

But there is more. When we celebrate Holy Communion we must focus on God's action in this world, what God has done for us in Christ. As sacramentalists, we look always for the presence of the LORD especially in baptism and Communion.

Jesus gave us two sacraments—Baptism and Communion--as means of receiving his grace. They are very special to every Christian.

Actually Baptism and Communion are closely linked together as they proclaim the story of God's work in our world. (Stookey) In baptism we, as the church, celebrate God's gift to us in Christ, cleansing us from past sin, welcoming us into the family of faith, and calling us to a new life in Christ, giving us a mission for Christ.

The Lord's Supper is a renewal of our baptism.

The supper also tells of God's work in our world through Jesus Christ. At the supper we are forgiven our sins and reminded of our calling in Christ.

As the travelers on the Road to Emmaus discovered, Christ was with them. As they thought back on that afternoon encounter with the stranger, they remembered how their entire persons had been changed by him. Suddenly their spirits, which had been gripped by the death of their dear friend, Jesus, had been lifted. They found that their hearts had even burned while the stranger was present.

They had not understood quite how it all happened, but it was a fact, the stranger had changed their lives! He had raised their spirits greatly. They were completely full of him, brimming over with news It was Jesus! They knew it instantly the minute he broke the bread. It was their LORD, who was with them!

They returned to their friends in the city. They had to share this marvelous news with the others right then. They had to tell their story of how they had just met Jesus on the road. They had to share their joy with the others.

As we've seen a great outpouring of God's love to us in the past few weeks, watching God's Spirit move many people to look and act beyond themselves. We can know God is present in our lives, in our nation, and in our world today.

That's what can happen for us. We, too, can experience Jesus' presence in the breaking of the bread.

Nutritionists have told us, "You are what you eat." I'm sure that's very true. Our bodies are completely dependent on the nutrients we offer them. If we eat only garbage or junk foods, if we drink or smoke or do drugs, our bodies will respond in like manner, and we can expect to have troubles.

We can choose to feed our spirits various foods, some are dangerous to us and some are healthy.

Bad spiritual food is pretty easy to figure—things that pray upon our spirits, that drag them down—immoral things—like pornographic material, breaking a sacred trust, indulging in addictive practices like gambling, seeking vengeance on someone, not forgiving someone. Those things will tear down your spirit and you will get sick.

On the other hand, our sacraments are good places for finding spiritually healthy food. Do you remember the words in from the Word and Table Service IV, spoken by the celebrant as he passed out the elements?

"Eat in your heart by faith with joy.

In remembrance that Christ died for thee, And feed on him in thy heart By faith with thanksgiving."

In our communion we can know that Christ is present with us. We can celebrate his love for us and experience him in the breaking and partaking of the bread.

www.ingramcontent.com/pod-product-compliance
Lightning Source LLC
LaVergne TN
LVHW051401080426
835508LV00022B/2916